The Future Association
of Taiwan with the
People's Republic of China

CHINA RESEARCH MONOGRAPH 22

INSTITUTE OF EAST ASIAN STUDIES
UNIVERSITY OF CALIFORNIA • BERKELEY
CENTER FOR CHINESE STUDIES

The Future Association of Taiwan with the People's Republic of China

Dan C. Sanford

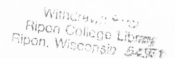

Although the Center for Chinese Studies, Institute of East Asian Studies, is responsible for the selection and acceptance of monographs in this series, responsibility for the opinions expressed in them and for the accuracy of statements contained in them rests with their authors.

Contents

Introduction

The United States, China, and Taiwan have all variously acknowledged that there is but one China. Reunification of the two Chinese areas has now been given added impetus by American normalization of relations with the People's Republic of China (PRC), but the question remains: What kind of association between the island of Taiwan and the mainland will there be and how will the connection occur? The official postnormalization positions of the Republic of China (ROC) and the People's Republic are far apart: The PRC appears ready to allow a large measure of autonomy for Taiwan if the government there drops its claim to sovereignty, but ROC officials are adamantly opposed to negotiations until the Chinese Communists abandon their adherence to Marxism-Leninism and establish a system of political freedoms and free enterprise.

Beneath the surface of officially stated positions, however, there are signals—in both words and actions—which suggest more favorable opportunities for accommodation. Strong arguments can be made that the foreign and domestic interests of the two governments are converging as the economic situation and the advances of Soviet and Vietnamese power transform relationships in East Asia. Domestically, China's drive for development through technology and modernization is parallelled by Taiwan's achievements in these areas. Putting politics and postures aside, the emerging economies of the two areas call for increased trade, aid, and cooperation.

Before we proceed in greater detail, we must settle an issue of terminology. The choice of terms used to describe the future relationship between Taiwan and the mainland significantly prejudices any analysis. The vocabulary used by the officials involved affects the politics of negotiation. The Chinese Communists have moved away from references to "liberation" and now talk about "reunification." "Liberation" usually meant the forceful eviction of the Kuomintang (KMT) from Taiwan, although, according to a recent finding, the late Zhou Enlai once interpreted the liberation of Taiwan in the same terms as the liberation of the mainland—to make the people of Taiwan their own masters.[a] "Reunification" is currently characterized

---

a. Ralph N. Clough, *Island China* (Cambridge: Harvard University Press, 1978), p. 137.

euphemistically as "autonomous status for a province under PRC sovereignty." Additionally, the term suggests that the two areas were formerly united, a point rarely disputed. To authorities in Taipei, the only positive word to use is "recovery" which, of course, implies transplanting the KMT-dominated government of the ROC to the mainland. In any other context, the Nationalists refer negatively to the "united front tactic," which recalls for them their long historical experience with Communist deceit and treachery.

Outside of China, various well-wishers hope that one China will be accomplished by means ranging from a "loose federation" to "integration"—perhaps the most extreme term for unification. While the former indicates considerable autonomy, the latter suggests full ties. Negotiations resulting in a concrete settlement between Beijing and Taipei, however, lie only in the realm of future surprises. Since political unification is unlikely, the word we can use to clarify most accurately the current trend is "association," an association of interests. It is safest to conclude from the most recent signs that the PRC may grow comfortable with mere legal and theoretical claims of sovereignty over Taiwan as long as it continues to derive increasingly substantial economic and strategic contributions from Taiwan and mutually friendly states. Full or real unification is not required. The fact that authorities in Beijing have for years allowed themselves to divorce their real foreign policies from the dictates of Marxist-Leninist theory testifies to their willingness to live with the superficial appearances— and the dichotomy between theory and reality.[b]

Whether this willingness applies in the case of Taiwan is a question crucially related to systemic changes arising from the unprecedented salience of domestic and international economic issues in the region. China's new sensitivity to economic goals and submission to an increasingly integrated global market system will result in decreasing concern with the political question of Taiwan. As economic and technological interdependence with the West causes a spill-over of interrelated interests across the Taiwan Strait, the nature of relations between Taiwan and the PRC may be more an economic question than a political one.

The following study assesses the measure by which Taiwan-China relations may evolve to an association which denies either full political unification or independence. It presents a perspective much neglected by analysts—i.e., the political impact of trade in the China theater. In early

---

b. This thesis knowingly contradicts Ralph Clough who wrote, "The citizens of the PRC would find it difficult to conceive of any solution to the Taiwan problem that did not ultimately make the island an integral part of China, in fact as well as in theory." Ibid., p. 123.

chapters of the monograph we question whether the optimistic forecasts of peaceful evolution in Taiwan-China relations is congruous with the evolving international system in East Asia. In this context the economic and political concerns shared by Taiwan and China are discussed. Taiwan's special effort to use foreign economic policy to overcome political obstacles is a crucial case in point for the argument that economic interests will come to bind Beijing and Taipei together.

Succeeding chapters show that Hong Kong (not Tibet, as some have suggested) is the most useful model to explain the probable direction for Taiwan. After outlining Hong Kong's peculiar arrangement with the mainland, attention is given to the ways in which Taiwan's case can parallel Hong Kong's. The theory of peaceful reconciliation between Taiwan and China assumes the continued moderation of policies on the mainland and new flexibility on Taiwan. Concluding chapters provide information supporting these assumptions.

I

Salience of Economics in the East Asian Political System

People who travel in East Asia and study the current Asian scene are likely to speak in unison about the profound new climate of practicality which seems to abound. The most noted feature of this pragmatism is that Asian actors—governmental and nongovernmental—have turned their attention to economic development. Nations which heretofore sought first to establish either national unification, domestic stability, or military security now seem uniformly ready to embrace material progress through active membership in the world economy. Not only has international trade accelerated at astounding speed for many of these countries, but their participation in transnational organizations has necessarily also risen. Asian cooperation on problems of development has entailed substantial growth in the organized processes and the institutional structures of the region.

If these impressions are supportable by fact in detail, then the emerging environment would seem to be one most beneficial for building positive connections between China and Taiwan. The reintegration of the People's Republic into the region's economy and into the world capitalist market has already effected fundamental changes in China's foreign policies.

Before saying more about these new conditions and China's role, we must examine two interrelated hypotheses common to functionalist theory. First, the international environment in the region may encourage positive economic interests when military/political conditions are stabilized. In this view of system change, the costs and risk in using force have nearly assured a disinclination to resort to force to change the status quo. The multiplicity of national interests, the fragility of new alignments, a confusion over the value of conventional warfare, and the deterrent effect of super weapons are all expected to render major conflicts unthinkable. Replacing an orientation of governments toward military security is a heightened level of sensitivity toward economic forces and economic constraints. Officials increasingly devote close attention to domestic and foreign economic planning because economics appear to be more important to future security and well-being.

1

The people of developing countries approaching the twenty-first century, moreover, are acquiring new central values of economic well-being, social justice, and ecological stability. Governments face constituents who are more cosmopolitan and more demanding of welfare services and consumer items.[1]

In the second hypothesis, the trend toward regional and global markets in the international environment produces an economically and technologically interpenetrated system which challenges the traditional insulation of national borders. International economic competition may take center stage, but this competition is generally seen as positive as long as countries succeed in diversifying exports and reaching certain international trade agreements. Leaders are discovering that economic growth and prosperity require trade, and trade requires correspondence, coordination of economic policies, and cooperation across borders. Under these circumstances, the perceived costs of traditional political competition and beggar-thy-neighbor policies are high, and a new premium is placed on low-level resolution of international issues that would otherwise impede progress in each burgeoning welfarist state.[2] The interdependence of national solutions to socioeconomic welfare problems leads invariably to international cooperation. No doubt this development is in part what functionalist writer David Mitrany has in mind when he writes that peaceful relations are "more likely to grow through doing things together in the workshop and marketplace than by signing pacts in chancelleries." To Mitrany, a kind of federalism of nations can occur by installments if political divisions can be overlaid with a "spreading web of international activities and agencies."[3]

Ernest B. Haas should also be credited with some of the initial statements popularizing this interpretation of what can happen in regions where member countries have made economic prosperity an a priori goal. Haas writes that as countries become increasingly devoted to their own social and economic welfare, they entrust tasks to experts. "Being interested in tasks rather than power, they can be expected to achieve agreement where statesmen will fail." Furthermore, Haas says, in the functionalist situation conflict is simply sidestepped as tasks are entrusted to agencies possessing functional rather than territorial jurisdiction. "If nations take full advantage of what, initially, are merely converging technical interests, eventually these interests will become fused." In the end, Haas concludes, nations will find themselves federated by the very force of things.[4]

---

1. A summary of this view may be found in James P. O'Leary, "Envisioning Interdependence: Perspectives on Future World Orders," *Orbis* 22 (Fall 1978): 507.
2. Ibid., p. 508.
3. Quoted by Ernest B. Haas, *Beyond the Nation State* (Palo Alto, Calif.: Stanford University Press, 1968), p. 11.
4. Ibid.

The Political/Military Environment

Does this vision really apply to China and the East Asian region? With some recent notable exceptions, the trend in the developing East Asian international system has been toward greater flexibility and multiplicity of interests. These features, in turn, enhance stability and allow countries to focus on important questions of economic welfare. Before the Vietnamese invasion and absorption of Kampuchea and the Chinese punishing invasion of Vietnam, observers optimistically characterized the system as stable and evolving toward an era of peaceful economic competition. As elsewhere on the globe, the value of military ventures seemed to be declining, while the advantages to be had from pragmatic, down-to-earth promotion of development seemed promising.[5] Robert Scalapino accurately describes the emerging system as one in which pervasive weakness and growing complexity in the political milieu now provide the restraints on violence and force which a balance of power alone could give before. "Subtly, the shift is now taking place from the psychological play of power to cost forces as key factors in restraint," Scalapino writes. "This in turn will gradually lead to new institutions of a suprastate type and, at the same time, induce support for some experiments cutting across regional lines."[6]

Detailed assessments of the military balance in East Asia are confusing at best. In the China case, Taiwan's "one-month" nuclear potential and gas warfare capability are thought to cancel the superiority in numbers and equipment of the People's Liberation Army.[7] The Koreas seem fairly well

---

5. Ralph N. Clough, *East Asia Security* (Washington, D.C.: Brookings Institution, 1975).

6. Robert Scalapino, "Intra-Asian Relations: An Overview," in *Intra-Asian International Relations*, ed. George T. Yu (Boulder, Colo.: Westview Press, 1977), p. 28. Scalapino discusses an alternate scenario of ineffective regionalism and threat of violence in the system. He concludes that the future lies somewhere between the two descriptions. Other observers, such as E. C. Ravenal, are not at all convinced that the future of the East Asia region is positive. Ravenal, for instance, predicts emergence of a dozen frustrated hegemonies with "surplus" political-military energies and competing goals. He contradicts the contention that technology will shrink distance, collapse regional compartments, and encourage homogeneous global concerns. "The New Strategic Balance in Asia," *Asia Pacific Community*, Fall 1978, p. 110.

7. The author recognizes a wide variance of opinion on this matter, but judges the preponderant attitude to be more favorable toward Taiwan's near-term security. Those most doubtful about Taiwan's equal position include Hungdah Chiu, "The Outlook for Taiwan," *Asian Affairs* 7 (January/February 1980): 141. Those who draw a more confident picture for Taiwan include Ralph N. Clough, *Island China* (Cambridge: Harvard University Press, 1978), and William R. Kintner and John F. Copper, *A Matter of Two Chinas* (Philadelphia: Foreign Policy Research Institute,

matched militarily, although the recent changes of government in the south suggest that the south may have a psychological disadvantage. American forces in South Korea may also make significant contribution to the stalemate. Japan's and America's supposed policy of equidistance between the U.S.S.R. and China, now tarnished by the close U.S.-China friendship and the Soviet intervention in Afghanistan, has perhaps at least kept the northeast military puzzle sufficiently complex to prevent any easy thought of useful military action there. In the southeast, the countries of ASEAN have cautiously sought to balance the military might of Vietnam through a united political front. Stanley Karnow concludes in *Foreign Affairs* that in East Asia, generally, complicated peace has been preferable to the ravages of war and that people are looking toward the future with increasing confidence and optimism.[8]

It is too early to say whether the warfare in Indochina in 1979 was a prelude to destabilization in the area and to an increase in the use of military force. The failure of China's "punishing" blow to the Vietnamese seems not to have undermined Chinese confidence in military force as a useful tool of national policy. China scholar Ross Terrill, for instance, finds no comfort in conversations with Chinese officials about the Vietnamese experience. He notes in his *Foreign Affairs* article on China in the 1980s that "there is little sign on the Chinese side of self-doubt, or of awareness of the ultimate futility of using military force to express anger toward a truculent small nation. . . . In no major nation does a strong antiwar movement seem less possible than in China."[9] Other sources seem convinced that China's foray into Indochina has, if anything, heightened Beijing's anxiety to modernize its armed forces and build an economy which can carry more massive military spending.[10]

An important, unpredictable, political/military feature thus remains in East Asia. We must conclude that it would be a mistake to rely on declining faith in the utility of force as a component of future peace in Asia. This conclusion does not rule out, however, a balance of power as an important stabilizing factor and the possible growing maturity of governments regarding cost/risk calculations. Most noteworthy in the China-Taiwan case is that mainland authorities are not confident about the results of a military encounter with Taiwan and seem unable to contemplate forceful action for some time to come.[11]

1979).

8. Stanley Karnow, "The Great Transformation in Asia, America and the World, 1978," *Foreign Affairs* 57 (Spring 1979): 612.

9. Ross Terrill, "China Enters the 1980's," *Foreign Affairs* 58 (Spring 1980): 925.

10. *Christian Science Monitor*, April 2, 1980.

11. *New York Times*, April 20, 1979.

Economic Environment

Economically, the East Asian region is brimming with potential. The area contains countries which have the most dynamic growth economies in the world and which are linked by increasingly sophisticated communications and transport systems. The Asia/Pacific basin has long replaced Western Europe as America's most important trading region. There is talk of a Pacific basin community which would promote free trade and transfers of capital in free and open, interdependent relations. At the center of this evolving system stand two important cities, Hong Kong and Singapore, whose goals are to serve as two financial and communications centers for the vast, new economic zone. ASEAN, though slow in coordinating economic policies, has proved that joint interest in promoting economic development can overcome diverse politics and cultures. Now ASEAN unity is giving its members effective bargaining muscle in trade negotiations with Japan, Australia, and the United States.[12]

Largely as a consequence of this expanded economic activity, international cooperation has been measurably enhanced. More than two dozen regional, intergovernmental organizations were created to meet international needs during the period 1950-1975. A majority of these organizations relate closely to functional economic issues. A study reported by James Schubert in *International Organization* proves conclusively just how important these organizations have become through the expansion of their scope and their tasks. According to Schubert, the Asian organizational system remains highly fragmented along geographical lines and has not yet reached the ideal functionalist "web" of associations overlaying numerous national divisions. Reflecting on the last two decades, however, Schubert finds that the functionalism in Asian regional cooperation has worked. He writes: "It may not be practically possible to completely remove the politics of welfare cooperation, but it is possible to structure from the cooperative setting to minimize the potential for obstructive politicization." The Asians have done this, he continues, by creating functionally specific institutions, by avoiding politics, by focusing on socioeconomic problems where possible, and by avoiding any

---

12. *Far Eastern Economic Review*, December 21, 1979, p. 54. The United States' focus on security in the region has been superseded by concerns for trade, technology transfer, and economic development. Trilateral Commission leaders several years ago saw the direction in which the East Asian region was moving and concluded that economy and market in command could be the mechanism for security in the Asian region. They were convinced that the attractions of the market economies and America's lead would strengthen the position of the United States and compensate for its decline in military strength. See Bruce Cummings, "The Political Economy of Chinese Foreign Policy," *Modern China* 5 (October 1979): 411.

challenge to sensitive areas of national sovereignty. Most pertinent to our hypothesis here is Schubert's conclusion that the prospect for cooperation cutting across East-West divisions appears to be a realistic possibility for the 1980s.[13] Smaller intraregional cooperatives, moreover, have a brighter future than the larger organizations requiring stronger central authority.[14]

China-Taiwan Case

The China-Taiwan arena does not match the model environment most suited to functional transformation. China and Taiwan are not officially two countries, but rather two areas in fact, and one country in theory. Moreover, mutual ideological references, usually presumed by functionalists to be a prior condition for functional integration, are almost totally absent. The two areas share a cultural affinity, and their perspectives of strategic security, aside from their own internecine conflict, are not far apart. Functionalists also stress that community comes from shared activity in welfare and economics. Welfare goals in Taiwan and the PRC may be similar, but the methods of reaching those goals have differed widely.

Some factors do nevertheless relate well to the functionalist theory. For one, it can be argued, the option to settle the Taiwan issue by force would seem to be practically canceled by the military standoff. The persistent disinterest of the People's Liberation Army in developing the capability for a significant amphibious attack is matched by the ROC's preparedness for annihilating attacking soldiers through gas warfare. The PRC's atomic weapons are matched by Taiwan's ability to deploy nuclear weapons after only one to two months' preparation. Putting aside the question of morale in Taiwan, military facts do not show the ROC's security to be a hostage to time. The PRC's superiority is not assured within another decade, if ever.

Economically, the two areas are not yet directly interdependent; they are rather becoming interdependent with common third countries. The interpenetration of foreign economies into Taiwan's economy is an intentional scheme of the ROC government. Taiwan constantly proclaims its success in using economics to overcome political obstacles and to enchance security (see chapter II).

The People's Republic of China has accepted the Western world's invitation to reenter the global market economy and has rapidly surmounted

---

13. James Schubert, "Toward a 'Working Peace System' in Asia: Organizational Growth and State Participation in Asian Regionalism," *International Organization* 32 (Spring 1978): 426, 459, 460.
14. Ibid., pp. 459-460.

immense ideological barriers built up over the previous twenty-five years of self-reliance. China's total trade in the 1970s grew by nearly 550 percent, with most growth occurring after 1972. Trade with the industrialized capitalist countries jumped from 46.8 percent to 64 percent during the ten-year period ending in 1975 and was expected to increase, given current contracts. In addition to this change, the traditional barter arrangements used by the PRC have given way to multiple capital acquisition arrangements such as the acceptance of export credits, foreign loans from both governmental and private sources, and joint ventures.[15] To some Westerners, China's entrance into the global economy provides the opportunity for a Communist nation to be tamed and controlled through induction into the world market (capitalist) system. As the famed Trilateral Commission puts it, bureaucratic degeneration of revolutionary socialism and the "strange and costly objects" of market economics will combine to bring China into the Western system. The pariah socialism will be disarmed.[16] Indeed, Marxist socialism is now under challenge in the People's Republic, and Chinese foreign policy has undergone a nearly complete reversal. For a while the policies of the "Gang of Four" successfully resisted China's incorporation into the new designs of Western capitalism. Jiang Qing, for one, was wary that China might be "letting the tiger in through the front door" by involvement with the market economies. She reportedly lamented that China's exports of oil had merely extricated capitalist countries from their energy crises. Wang Hongwen supposedly complained that the foreign trade department was betraying the national interest. Zhang Chunqiao objected to China's new approach to the capitalist economies as "going in for a colonial economy."[17] For the time being, these apprehensions are in disrepute. The policy of self-reliance is not dead, but current economic planners seem far along the way to causing its demise. The accumulated reports of today's economic activities between China and foreign capitalist areas in North America and Europe contribute convincingly to the notion that China's economy will be integrated into a market in which Taiwan is already fully entwined.[18]

---

15. Greg O'Leary, "China Comes Home: The Re-integration of China into the World Economy," *Journal of Contemporary Asia* 9 (1979): 467.

16. See Cummings, "The Political Economy," *Modern China* 5 (October 1979): 452-453.

17. Ibid., p. 411.

18. Greg O'Leary writes, "With their [the Gang of Four] demise, however, new trading and investment relationships, new political alliances under the banner of opposition to social-imperialism and the severance of political ties which remained hostile to the perspectives being developed in the West, led to the institutionalization of policies which have decisively altered China's international relations." In "China Comes Home," p. 474.

The mainland has also admitted being attracted to Taiwan as a model of development and modernization and can be expected to increase its interest in trade with that area simultaneously with expanded Sino-Western trade. The PRC's new reliance on Western loans and major Western corporations to provide technological services and equipment is matched by Taiwan's long experience in using foreign investments and sizable exports for economic survival. The expectation is that China's new interdependence with Europe, Japan, and North America will unavoidably draw that country into the same business circles long associated with the ROC. While China's leaders will naturally resist crippling dependence on the Western economy, China's economic association with the West is likely to be strong enough that those leaders would not want to do anything to injure the stability of the Pacific/Asian economic system or its particular business partners. While China's major trading partners continue to serve as Taiwan's major trading partners, it would not be in China's self-interest to invade Taiwan or in any way disturb its favorable economic climate. We thus conjecture that brisk economic exchange in Asia may someday disarm the political hostility between Beijing and Taipei. Such a conjecture would seem particularly true in a regional atmosphere of cooperation dominated by governments, planners, and businessmen, all driven to achieve material progress for themselves and their countrymen. It will next be constructive to see how Taiwan has responded to recent challenges and taken full advantage of the concerted interest in economic growth among its neighbors.

II

Taiwan's Strategy of Economics Over Politics

Japan is one of the first countries to have forged the path of economics over politics in recent times. It has become the pacifist's prize model of a major economic power surviving with little attention to the military challenge posed by its chief competitors. In Japan's case, developing a military force was neither an option nor a necessity because of America's postoccupation alliance. While not always succeeding in the first try, Japan has managed generally to separate politics from economics in its relations with the Middle East, Southeast Asia, the two Chinas, and the Soviet Union. In some cases, such as various Middle East crises, Japan's conciliation seemed beyond mere diminution of political considerations; it appeared to some as total disregard for international principle at the expense of allies.

Of special interest is Japan's policy toward the two Chinas and the response of the Chinese on both sides. Japan's businessmen were trading with the mainland Chinese as early as the 1950s. From that time up to the establishment of diplomatic relations with the People's Republic of China in 1972, both Taiwan and the PRC forbade their Japanese clients from engaging in business with their opposition. Japan, however, was increasingly able to overcome this obstacle by creating corporate subsidiaries whose connections were hard to trace. Eventually, blacklisting from Taipei or Beijing proved fruitless.

Just as the PRC had generally accommodated Japan's continued investment and trade with Taiwan before 1972, Taiwan promptly opted for continued economic relations with Japan after diplomatic relations were reversed. With the so-called Japanese formula, Taiwan hosted the Interchange Association from Japan, which was to assume the tasks ordinarily handled by a consulate. Judging by the results in trade, travel, and investment, neither side has suffered from the Japanese formula. Trade volume with both Taiwan and China has improved during the last nine years, fluctuating according to changes in market conditions. Agreements about air and shipping service were the most difficult to conclude. It was finally decided to give a new name to the Japanese airlines that would fly to Taipei and to separate PRC and ROC aircraft and ships at Japanese ports. In each case, the Chinese parties first insisted that the other be excluded from Japan but later set aside politics and pride to derive maximum profit from the Japanese market.[1]

From this earlier flirtation with the concept of "economics over politics," the ROC has advanced to a stage in which international trade is promoted as a policy that guarantees international existence. Maximum interdependence among the ROC, the U.S., Japan, and some 140 other nations, authorities must have reasoned, would become as important to Taiwan's defense and security as its 500,000 armed forces or its supplies of weapons. While the government might lose ambassadorial relations with all but a few of the world's nations, it would survive through economic involvement. While reduced to a "political vegetable," it could remain active in the world of international economic relations. After all, they must have calculated, no government in this era of critical economic balance can flippantly choose policies that risk serious loss of investment or disruption of important business abroad. Taiwan's self-determination will come to be defended by countless countries and businessmen who have decided that money really counts for power.

Thus with great gusto Taiwan set out in the 1970s to generate business ties and foreign investment, in the process endearing itself to many powerful interests. Since the Shanghai Communique between the U.S. and the PRC, Taiwan's foreign trade has increased by at least 300 percent; it now contributes to more than 50 percent of the island's total gross national product. The phenomenal 30 percent annual growth in foreign trade has brought the ROC into the front ranks of the world's major trading countries (sixteenth largest exporting country in the world in 1978). The ROC has been second only to Japan and well ahead of Hong Kong, Korea, and Singapore in gross exports of goods. Much of this increase can be attributed to a clear governmental effort on the part of Taiwan to eliminate red tape and delays for foreign investors. In a number of major decisions in 1977, the ROC economics ministry simplified administrative procedures, increased the permissible annual repatriation of capital to 20 percent of the original investment, eased entry and exit regulations for foreign and local businessmen, provided certain new business tax exemptions, and provided foreigners with more information about investment opportunities. The policies could hardly have been more pointedly directed toward achieving a rapid expansion of business.[2]

---

1. See Ralph N. Clough, *Island China* (Cambridge: Harvard University Press, 1978), pp. 173-201.
2. *Free China Review*, January 1978, p. 25 (hereafter *FCR*).

Trade with Japan

Japan and the United States continue to be the prime investors in the ROC economy. In Japan's case, Taiwan has made special invitation to assorted small investors—persons who could not easily recover should Taiwan lose its bid for autonomy. Japan's derecognition of the ROC did account for temporary reduction in the flow of yen into the island; now, however, Japanese bankers, traditionally shy of major syndicated loans to Taiwan, are looking at the local lending market.[3]

Two-way trade between the countries was scarcely affected by the break in diplomatic relations. Japan has seen a rising curve in its trade with Taiwan, and up to the present the value of that trade has either kept abreast of Japan-PRC trade or has surpassed it. Japanese exports to Taiwan continually exceed exports to the PRC. Japan's two-way trade with Taiwan in 1976, for example, totaled $3.5 billion.[4] Large numbers of Japanese tourists continue to visit Taiwan. Japan has kept the trade surplus with Taiwan and, thus, continues to be the dominant partner. ROC officials can nonetheless exert considerable influence on those in Japan who appreciate the advantages which Japan derives from its trade with the island. The Japanese Foreign Ministry has remained sensitive to the needs of the ROC and will accommodate its political demands as much as possible without provoking the PRC.[5]

Trade with the United States

The United States has been Taiwan's primary export recipient and has been second only to Japan in providing the ROC's imports. Even knowledge of the impending Shanghai Communique did not dampen the United States' eagerness to expand trade, credit, and investment with the ROC. The U.S. State Department continued to give tacit encouragement to businessmen even when normalization with the PRC was certain.

At the U.S. State Department before normalization with China, authorities were convinced that the most important condition to consider in negotiations with the PRC was the right to continue and even accelerate economic ties with Taiwan. They believed that Taiwan's future would be guaranteed because Beijing would not want to jeopardize its own budding ties with American investors and corporations. During and after normalization,

---

3. Bill Kazer, "Making the Best of Reality," *Far Eastern Economic Review,* May 18, 1979, p. 28 (hereafter *FEER*).
4. Clough, *Island China,* p. 194.
5. Ibid.

American corporations that had previously been established in Taiwan (such as RCA, Union Carbide, Gulf Oil, and General Instrument Corporation) continued or even expanded their manufacturing investments, while major new participants in auto, electronics, oil, and agribusiness industries were planning to enter the market. Rather than being disheartened by U.S. derecognition of Taiwan, American businessmen reported a sense of relief that the "air was finally clear" and that business could continue as usual.[6]

American bankers proved so eager to lend money to Taiwan at one point that they had driven interest rates on loans down to the lowest in Asia. Taiwan's indebtedness to the United States EXIM bank has made it that bank's third largest customer. One source has noted that the ROC's borrowing is clearly bigger than it need be, considering the country's impressive growth and domestic savings. The ROC's credit rating remained strong in 1979, and the NT dollar continued to gain prestige in the Asian market along with the currencies of Japan, Hong Kong, and Singapore. Needless to say, EXIM and the other major lenders in Taiwan—Citibank, Chase Manhattan, Irving Trust, and Bank of America—have no intention of leaving the ROC. National Bank of Chicago's exit from Taipei in late 1977 to conclude a transaction with the PRC proved the single exception.

In its trade promotion, the ROC seems clearly determined to garner American friendship by sharply increasing imports. While the ROC has already achieved considerable status as the eighth ranking trade partner of the U.S., Taiwan's authorities seem to believe that capturing an even larger share of America's trade can only help Taiwan's future security. In an apparent attempt to dramatize Taiwan's crucial role in America's economic future and to win maximum goodwill in the United States, the ROC government sent several purchasing missions to America in 1978-1979. To have these groups of Chinese businessmen travel from state to state signing purchase contracts amounting to a total of U.S. $25 million was likely to make a greater impression than all the propaganda and advertising of the ROC embassy during that period. As photographers snapped away at Taiwan trade officials signing purchase orders for American products, ranging from bulk commodities to heavy machinery, the island's importance to the U.S. economy was forcefully driven home.[7]

---

6. Roy Rowan, "Taiwan Gears Up to Go It Alone," *Fortune*, February 12, 1979, p. 74. Also, in *Free China Weekly,* September 23, 1979, p. 1, Anthony Greayher, Pacific regional manager of the British-based Grindlay's Bank, was quoted as saying, "The air has been cleared and the uncertainty is gone. The name of the game may be changed but the business continues" (hereafter *FCW*).
7. See Chen Pin, "Trading with the Americans," *FCR*, November 1979, p. 19.

The missions also served to narrow the trade balance gap, which had been in Taiwan's favor. Americans cannot help but feel grateful to a country which goes out of its way to redress a trade balance in America's favor. Moreover, giving high visibility to large block purchases reinforces the psychological impact of major PRC contract offers to U.S. companies. As a consequence of the ROC's buying missions and other steps such as lifting the ban on the import of passenger automobiles (solely for the benefit of North American manufacturers), imports from the United States rose by 36 percent in 1979. This increase, along with the 11.8 percent increase in the ROC's exports to America, makes U.S.-ROC trade volume about seven times that of the U.S.-PRC trade, a ratio calculated in January 1979.[8]

European and Other Markets

Trade with Europe (14 percent of the total) has been brisk, even though no European country recognizes Taiwan. Taiwanese companies have aggressively marketed products in the EEC by working through the consular and embassy substitute organizations, the China External Trade Development Council, and the Far East Trade Service, Inc. U.S. derecognition has apparently had the same positive effect on European business interests in Taiwan as it has had on American interests. Tremendous headway has been made with France, which was one of the original PRC sympathizers and which recognized the mainland government in the early 1960s. Exports to France in the first five months of 1979 were up 52 percent compared to the same period in 1978.[9] On the basis of these statistics, the ROC government has called upon manufacturers and traders in Taiwan to increase their purchases from France to aid that country in its trade balance. Taiwan executives have also been busy in England. The Tatung Company, Taiwan's largest electronics manufacturer, for instance, announced in December 1980 that it had arranged to take over the operation of an English television plant belonging to Decca. This plant would give Tatung a long-sought-after foothold in the PAL-system TV market in Europe.[10] Some thought has also been given to organizing additional purchasing groups in more nations in Europe and in Canada to help coax other nations into thinking more seriously about the value of links with Taipei.[11] Recent European investments on the island

---

8. Ibid., p. 21.
9. *FCW*, September 30, 1979, p. 1.
10. A report on the ROC-France trade in *FCW*, September 30, 1979, added, "An increase in two-way trade will help strengthen relations between the two countries in other fields." See also *FCW*, December 14, 1980, p. 34.
11. *FEER*, May 18, 1979, p. 28.

have been made by such companies as N. V. Phillips of the Netherlands, Grundig of West Germany, ICI (chemicals), and General Electric Company of the United Kingdom. Several years ago the GEC won a major contract to electrify Taiwan's railways, even though the GEC of England also acquired mainland business, and its chairman, Lord Nelson, headed the Sino-British Trade Council, which promotes trade with the mainland.[12] Great Britain's trade partnership with Taiwan had been encouraged by the Anglo-Taiwan Trade Committee established in 1976 and more recently strengthened by the decision of Grindlay's Bank of Britain to become the first European bank to open a branch in Taiwan. This growing relationship is particularly surprising given the dramatic role British businessmen have been playing in the booming Hong Kong-PRC investment and trade projects. Other European banks now having branches in Taiwan include Hollandsche Bank-Unie of the Netherlands, Banque de Paris et de Pays-Bas of France, and the German-run Euro-Pacific Bank.

Aside from Europe, Saudi Arabia and Kuwait in the Middle East and Brazil, Guatemala, Venezuela, Panama, Argentina, Chile, Ecuador, Mexico, and Columbia in Latin America have become close trading partners in recent years. Saudi Arabia, one of only twenty-one nations that retain formal diplomatic relations with the ROC, is of particular interest because it is the last major country to recognize and support the ROC. Taiwan's roughly $300 million worth of exports to Saudi Arabia make Saudi Arabia Taiwan's best customer in the Middle East. To retain close ties, the ROC has in some cases taken from the Saudis large contracts that it knows are unprofitable. In 1980 Taiwan extended its dependence on Saudi Arabia by accepting several major loans for developing energy resources. Of course, Taiwan appreciates the dependable supply of oil which Saudi Arabia offers. The PRC also finds itself attracted to Saudi Arabia as a bulwark against Soviet influence in the Middle East and as a possible supplier of development capital. PRC exports to Saudi Arabia in recent years have totaled about $25 million annually.[13]

With all this activity, it is not surprising that in the first half of 1979 the ROC continued to register a 30 percent overall increase in two-way trade. Overseas investments in the ROC in 1979 represented a 155 percent increase over the previous year. In the first eight months of 1980, overseas investments in Taiwan increased 24.47 percent over 1979.[14]

Even more dramatic are Taiwan's foreign investments by private firms. The government's liberalization, designed to encourage such disbursements abroad, has resulted in a six-fold increase in the first five months of 1980

12. *Wall Street Journal*, March 25, 1977 (hereafter *WSJ*).
13. *Christian Science Monitor*, November 2, 1979 (hereafter *CSM*).
14. *FCW*, October 19, 1980, p. 4.

compared to 1979. The major recipients of Taiwan's capital are the United States, Singapore, Indonesia, Saudi Arabia, and Paraguay.[15]

Like many aspiring mini-powers, the ROC has also discovered the psychological boost that can be derived from having a successful national airline. China Airlines finally surmounted the PRC pressures against Japan and recovered its profitable flights to that country. Additionally, in recent years China Airlines has been adding flights to Singapore, Manila, and Saudi Arabia. The ROC, having secured new landing rights in Luxembourg, is also set on a course of rapid expansion in Europe. Similar privileges have been under negotiation in France, Germany, Belgium, and Turkey. In France the ROC is bargaining for CAL entrance with an offer to buy French-made airliners. In a world in which airline flights have often been interpreted as showing support or at least interconnection, ROC officials must be thinking that the CAL flagships' landing frequently in major world capitals proves the vitality of Taiwan's economy and the extensive nature of its friendships.

Largely as a consequence of these developments in Taiwan's international business, many nations with embassies in Beijing have moved to establish closer governmental ties with Taiwan as well. Among those turning back for more semiofficial relations are Japan, France, West Germany, Belgium, Spain, Singapore, Ecuador, and Jordan.[16]

Implications

Naturally, rising prosperity in Taiwan is valuable for a number of reasons, aside from the strategic advantages in garnering foreign friends. Economic growth enhances domestic stability and encourages confidence in the KMT-dominated government. In foreign affairs, such growth helps compensate for the many diplomatic setbacks of recent years. Economic expansion may have been one of only a few options, yet the Chinese government on Taiwan proved it could accommodate to the new range of pressures and effectively lead its people into exploiting new opportunities. As one local banker put it, "An industrialized country's attracting foreign capital is our best guarantee for the future."[17] Now, too many countries have interests in Taiwan for the island's immediate future to be compromised.

---

15. Phil Kurata, "Searching for New Friends Abroad," *FEER*, August 8, 1980, pp. 44-45.
16. J. Bruce Jacobs, "Taiwan 1979: 'Normalcy after Normalization,' " *Asian Survey* 20 (January 1980): 86.
17. Bill Kazer, "Making the Best of Reality," *FEER*, May 18, 1979, p. 28. For similar reaction, see Phillippe Pons, "The Taiwan Dilemma," *Atlas World Press Review*, September 15-17, 1978, p. 18.

One feature of Taiwan's elevated position in the international business community which has the most far-reaching ramifications for its relations with mainland China is the number of foreign corporations that have chosen to invest simultaneously in both areas. Businessmen have become the largest group of transnational participants in the Taiwan-China area and are having some effect on the attitudes of both sides. We know that China and Taiwan today are sharing basically the same trading partners. Statistics indicate that Taiwan's most important business partners are the United States, Japan, Hong Kong, Kuwait, and West Germany, in that order. Saudi Arabia is moving up quickly on the list, as are several other European countries of the EEC. China's important business partners are Japan, Hong Kong, the United States, and West Germany, with Australia and Canada following close behind, and Saudi Arabia just now joining the list.[18] The only significant differences, then, regarding which foreigners Taiwan and China find useful to their economies are that Taiwan must rely much more on Arabs for its petroleum and that in the China market, Japan has had a head start over the United States. Also, China continues small trade with Eastern Europeans and the Russians, people who have been absent from Taiwan, which is just now entering the Eastern European market.

This information suggests that new brokers, who represent a few major countries, have emerged into a position from which they may effectively bridge differences across the Taiwan Straits. It would be helpful to know which companies in these five or six major countries are involved and what types of relations their key executives have with the political leadership in both Chinese areas. An investigation of this sort would be far too exhaustive for this study, but the situation for some American companies, besides being more easily appraised, may also illumine the previous suggestion. Comparing the list of member firms of the National Council for U.S.-China Trade with the most recent compilation by the World Trade Academy Press of American firms in Taiwan shows that at least thirty-eight corporations are currently conducting or proposing business with both the Nationalists and the Communist Chinese. (Undoubtedly, the actual figure is much higher, since both lists are incomplete.) Only a handful of these corporations appears to have established any substantial business with both Taiwan and the People's Republic of China. In this group are Bank of America, Ford Motor Company, Gulf Oil Corporation, International Telephone and Telegraph, 3M Company, Fluor Corporation, Sea-Land Service, Inc., Chase Manhattan Bank, RCA, U.S. Steel International, General Motors, Union Carbide, American Express, and Kodak.

---

18. *China: International Trade Quarterly Review*, Second Quarter 1979, A Research Paper, January 1980, p. 5; Michel Oksenberg, "China Policy for the 1980's," *Foreign Affairs* 59 (Spring 1981): 305.

Only a few of the U.S. firms attempting to do business with both countries have experienced any difficulty with Chinese authorities regarding their dual role. In three cases, American firms (First National Bank of Chicago, Pan American World Airways, and Gulf Oil Corporation) felt obliged either to withdraw from one Chinese market altogether or to call upon a subsidiary to save embarrassment for one side or the other. However, in each of these situations these maneuvers were decided upon as early as 1977, well before the U.S.-China normalization. At that time, the requirements for a foothold in the China market were yet unclear, and dual roles were not tried and tested.[19] Some other businesses in those years before normalization had apparent success with roving operations. Chief representatives for Sea-Land Corporation in Taiwan, for instance, took on the task of negotiating shipping contracts with PRC officials in Hong Kong. A Sea-Land executive in Taipei simply flew to Hong Kong and returned to Taiwan with the full knowledge of the ROC government.

Today such activity is common. Many American companies still maintain separate divisions or subsidiaries to deal with Taiwan and China, but they no longer schedule separate trips for their executives in Asia. While it is still unusual for the same executives to be assigned both to Taipei and Beijing simultaneously because the companies are generally not looking at the same market or the same products in both areas, those who are handed assignments in both areas seem to shuttle in and out of Hong Kong to ports of disembarkation in Taiwan or China without difficulty. Two recent cases underline the extent of relaxation in Chinese attitudes toward these occurrences. In April 1980, *New York Times* reporter James Sterba recounted that Dr. An Wang, founder and president of Wang Laboratories, went from a meeting with President Chiang Ching-kuo and other senior Kuomintang officials in Taiwan to China after only a short stopover in Hong Kong. In China, Dr. Wang discussed with officials possible joint ventures with his computer company. In another surprising case, Robert P. Parker, president of the American Chamber of Commerce on Taiwan, left his residence in Taipei to attend the opening of the American Consulate in Canton with Vice-president Mondale and returned to Taiwan without recrimination.[20]

---

19. Melinda Liu, "Loyalty and Rock-bottom Terms," *FEER*, June 22, 1979, pp. 98-99. See also "Taiwan and the Foreign Investor," *Pacific Affairs* 50 (Winter 1977): 644-657. First National Bank of Chicago became the first U.S. bank to make a direct loan to China with a modest $8 million credit to purchase coastal shipping vessels. *WSJ*, June 7, 1979.

20. James Sterba, "China and Taiwan Urging US to Trade with Both," *NYT*, April 9, 1980.

In countless additional instances American businessmen demonstrated sufficient agility and the Chinese sufficient pragmatism that companies have bargained with both sides without jeopardy. RCA has negotiated the sale of color television sets to Beijing while engaged in the highly successful manufacture of television sets in Chungli, Taiwan. In Hong Kong, Bank of America officials arranged joint financing with the PRC's Bank of China while the company's senior vice-president told a conference in Taipei that Bank of America and "leading banks from all over the free world" regard the Republic of China as a "most welcome customer."[21] After Henry Ford II and the Ford Motor Company's executive vice-president visited China in 1978, Ford Motor Company concluded a sale of seven hundred trucks and initiated talks with the People's Republic for the sale of commercial vehicles, agricultural tractors, even complete auto plants. Meanwhile, in Taipei, Raymond C. F. Chen, president of Ford Lio Ho Motor Company, announced that his Detroit bosses encouraged him to proceed with a ten-year expansion plan as a way of expressing confidence in the Republic of China.[22] Recently, the Eli Lilly International Corporation invited a business management delegation from the People's Republic of China to tour the Lilly corporate headquarters in Indianapolis and participate in a seminar with Lilly executives. During the same time in late 1979, a representative from corporate headquarters visited the Taiwan affiliate of the Lilly Corporation in Taiwan as part of an official Indiana state delegation for the purpose of signing a "sister-state" agreement between Indiana and Taiwan. According to a spokesman from the Lilly Corporation, the firm will continue to support its employees in Taiwan even while exploring trade possibilities with the PRC and cooperating in technical and business seminars with Chinese from the mainland.[23]

The reasons for mainlander openness to these overlapping arrangements and even encouragement for U.S. companies to integrate their mainland and Taiwan operations will be discussed in the next chapter. Kuomintang leaders on Taiwan appear willing to encourage American companies to go comparison shopping on the mainland because they believe that Taiwan's efficiency, quality, and incentives will in the long run prove more attractive.[24]

---

21. *FCW*, November 11, 1979, p. 4. Bank of America reported in 1979 receiving approval in Beijing to establish a full banking relationship with the Bank of China. *FCW*, January 24, 1979, p. 10.
22. *CSM*, November 30, 1978.
23. *FCW*, November 11, 1979, p. 4. See also Roy Rowan, "Taiwan Gears Up to Go It Alone," *Fortune*, February 12, 1979, p. 73.
24. Of the twelve company representatives questioned by this researcher, none foresaw the triangular relationship between Taipei and Beijing and the transnational companies changing the basic objectives and differences between Taiwan and the PRC. However, there was consensus that the willingness of each side to tolerate a company's connection with the other was highly encouraging.

Regardless of the rationale on either side, these companies' joint interest and expanding activities in both Chinas would seem to create an environment of trust and appreciation between their Chinese clients.

III

Shared Strategic Concerns of the PRC and the ROC

Most commentaries on the China-Taiwan issue begin with the premise that the countries are adversaries and that their mutual hostility is unalterable. While this assumption seems only natural, given the declarations of President Chiang Ching-kuo in Taiwan and the general PRC opposition to Kuomintang rule on the island, both sides have begun to face the realities of the changing balance of power in Asia following the American defeat in Vietnam. While transformations are ignored in public, Chinese in both areas can be observed occasionally acting or speaking in concert. Denials to the contrary and claims of doubt about vastly changed circumstances in Asia should not preclude some exploration of the ways in which China and Taiwan may in time share some common concerns.

Chinese nationalism, the driving force for unity and national defense against imperialism, is a singular ideological reality for both camps. Historically, the outside challenges to China's integrity have inspired nationalism in both Chinese groups and have brought temporary united fronts between the KMT and the Chinese Communist Party. As a matter of fact, the Nationalist Chinese were at one point only slightly less critical of America's negative contribution to China's search for international status and justice than were the Communist Chinese.[1] Both parties have sought the help of the United States in building China. Both parties have received aid from the Soviet Union to defend Chinese interests against foreign imperialists. Chiang Kai-shek enlisted Soviet help against Japan during World War II; and, of course, Mao Zedong contracted for Soviet assistance during and after China's war with the United States in Korea.

With regard to national minorities, Beijing and Taipei have held similar Chinese prejudices. During the People's Republic's forceful campaigns to

---

1. See Dan C. Sanford, "The Nationalist Predisposition Towards the United States," (Ph.D. diss., University of Denver, 1971).

20

restore Tibet to Chinese sovereignty, the Nationalist Chinese harbored refugees from the broken territory; however, these persons who escaped from Tibet were not invited to the ROC as freedom fighters deserving independence for their country. Rather, they were received as a Chinese minority joining compatriots on the island in the fight against Communist traitors in "Peiping." The ROC objected to Beijing's efforts to dominate the small Himalayan territory because it was the Communists who would be the governors and not because the area was suffering incorporation into China.

Neighboring Areas

Similarly, both the ROC and the PRC oppose Vietnam's expansion in Indochina. Hanoi's eviction of Vietnamese of Chinese origin and its extension of direct power into Kampuchea have drawn heavy criticism from both Chinese capitals. Taipei had long hoped to join the war against the Vietnamese Communists during America's presence there and later responded to Vietnam's actions by inviting refugees to take residence in Taiwan. Taipei's response to China's war of "punishment" against Vietnam early in 1979 was surprisingly calm. Most newspapers preferred to set aside the issue of whether China's action was justified or not; they chose instead to use the news as illustration that Peking was unpredictable and not averse to using force.

In the case of Japan, both areas have now settled World War II claims and signed a peace agreement. Taiwan has been challenged to improve its negative imbalance of trade with Japan and also prod Japan into constraining Taiwanese independence movements which sometimes arise in that country. China has been challenged to prevent its economy from becoming unduly dependent on Japan. The PRC also has expressed anxiety over any encouragement of "two Chinas" emanating from Japan. Both Chinas claim sovereignty over the Ryukyus Islands now administered by Japan. To show their determination to achieve eventual control, the mainland Chinese sent a fleet of fishing boats into the vicinity of the Senkaku Islands in the Ryukyu chain during the spring of 1978. While little came of this demonstration, Beijing had at least made its intentions clear to the Japanese. Some may remember that in 1970, after East China Sea surveys indicated the possibility of petroleum deposits near the Senkakus, the Nationalists also asserted Chinese sovereignty over these islets by sending a gunboat to plant a flag there and by building the issue into a small crisis with Japan. After Okinawan officials removed the flag, members of Taiwan's National Assembly visited the island. There was talk of an armed confrontation, and the Nationalists repeated warnings that only Chinese had the right to pursue petroleum explorations there.[2]

---

2. William Glenn, "Cool Line on the Senkaku 'Bandits,' " *Far Eastern Economic Review,* May 5, 1979, p. 33 (hereafter *FEER*).

Sino-Soviet Relations

The United States' competition with the Soviet Union affects both Taiwan and China. The expanding Soviet power and influence, particularly in Africa, South Asia, and the Middle East, accompanied by significant American retrenchment, worries Chinese Communist and non-Communist alike. For the People's Republic, this situation is so threatening that it calls for pragmatic policies regardless of ideological costs. It requires a direct carrot-and-stick approach to Moscow, on the one hand, and maximum encouragement of anti-Soviet groups in Europe, Africa, the Middle East, and Asia, on the other hand. This Soviet menace is said to have rushed China into dropping previous conditions in order to speed normalization with the United States. Before normalization a CCP official surprised correspondents by commenting that perhaps the PRC would be willing to have the United States "guard" Taiwan for China for the time being.[3] Then in 1979, Chairman Hua Guofeng indicated his willingness to shelve almost all differences with America to insure Chinese economic growth and to cope with the far more serious Soviet problem. He even implied that the United States might continue to supply some arms to the ROC without jeopardizing the normalization process.[4] Observers consequently now face the confusing and unusual prospect of the United States' simultaneously announcing a sale of arms to Taiwan and discussing military assistance to the PRC.[5] Neither Taipei nor Beijing favors a further decline in America's military posture in the Asia/Pacific region, except, in the PRC's view, in South Korea.

---

3. See references to speech by Geng Biao, Director of the International Liaison Department of the Central Committee of the Chinese Communist Party; in James Hsiung, "US Relations with China in the Post-Kissingerian Era," *Asian Survey* 17 (August 1977): 703.

4. A study by John M. Newman reported as follows: "On December 5, Deng summoned Woodcock [Leonard] and stated he would, 'though very reluctantly,' cause no uproar about the extra year of the U.S.-Taiwan defense treaty and continued arms purchases. (Evans and Novak, *Washington Post,* December 18, 1978). It was left to Hua to deal with the substantive U.S. demand on arms sales, which he did in the joint communique of December 16 by stating that while China 'can absolutely not agree' to continued arms sales, such sales would not preclude normalization." John Michael Newman, "The Chinese Succession Struggle," *Asian Affairs* 6 (January/February 1979): 180.

5. Also in 1979 Deng Xiaoping told American senators that China would like to see an expanded United States naval presence in the Western Pacific and more defense coordination by the Southeast Asian countries. *New York Times,* January 10, 1979 (hereafter *NYT*). See also U.S., Congress, Senate, Committee on Foreign Relations, *Sino-American Relations: A New Turn,* (Washington, D.C.: Government Printing Office, January 1979), pp. 3-4.

The ROC's reaction to Soviet advances in Asia has not been consistent. While continually pledging opposition to Communism anywhere, whether in "Peiping" or Moscow, Nationalist leaders have sometimes refrained from heaping as much scorn on the Russians as on the Chinese Communists. In fact, a dramatic whitewashing of the Soviets appears to have taken place in ROC literature during the years when the Sino-Soviet division became clear to all. Before 1960, Mao Zedong was branded a puppet of Moscow, a Russian lackey in Chinese disguise. The U.S.S.R. was the principal Communist villain. After the 1960s, Mao Zedong, personally, received the brunt of Taiwan's attacks. The Soviet Union was placed in increasingly better light by Nationalist commentators not because of any official recognition that Russian foreign policies had become harmless, but because Communist China's "warmongering" had surpassed the Soviet Union's.[6]

According to Madame Chiang Kai-shek, the Russians had through "gradualism" moved away from Marxism-Leninism and only continued to give these doctrines "lip service" for fear of being bested by the Chinese Communists.[7] These words have crucial implications. First, if Beijing really had been determined to involve the Soviets in a war which would leave Russian manpower sharply depleted by "terrific attrition and wholesale carnage by atom and hydrogen warheads," then one might infer that the People's Republic was primarily responsible for the conflicts of the 1950s. Did the madame mean to suggest that in Korea, for example, Mao had attempted to entangle Russia in a general war?[8] This would mean that the Soviets were not nearly so aggressive as they had been portrayed. Rather, they had been innocently dragged into conflicts which the People's Republic had instigated. Was this a reinterpretation of history? Were the Nationalists clearing a path for a possible future attempt to exonerate the Soviets from their previous crimes?

Second, the energy with which Nationalist spokesmen drew attention to Russia's new enemy, Beijing, suggests that the Nationalists foresaw a mutual interest developing between them and the Russians in ridding China of Mao and his supporters. If indeed the Soviets through gradualism were no longer

---

6. *Free China Review,* November 1965, p. 86, and February 1966, p. 86 (hereafter *FCR*).
7. Madame Chiang Kai-shek, *Selected Speeches 1965-1966* (Taiwan: China Publishing Co., 1968), pp. 50, 71-72, 99, 156-157, 198-199, 204, 205-206.
8. In an address delivered to the World Affairs Council on October 19, 1966, Madame Chiang said, "We must also remember that it was Mao who in the 1970's tried to inveigle Russia into a general war in the belief that Russia would then have to give her the *savoir-faire* scientific data to atomic weaponry through meshing of Soviet and Red Chinese military operations and the *sine qua non* needed to Red Chinese cooperation." Madame Chiang Kai-shek, *Selected Speeches 1965-1966.*

genuine Marxist-Leninists, as was being said, better relations might not be so unthinkable.[9]

Obviously, there were limits to Nationalist China's infatuation with Russia during this period. Although recognizing that a reciprocal interest between the Soviet Union and the "free world" might assist in isolating Communist China and substituting leadership there, the Nationalist Chinese still asserted that such reciprocity could not last very long. It was said that once the Soviets succeeded in toppling Mao from power and replacing him with a milder, pro-Soviet, leader, they would revert to their basic plan of expansion.[10]

As the Cultural Revolution waned and as border clashes brought the Soviet Union and mainland China to the brink of war, the Nationalists again allowed rumors of possible relations with the Soviet Union. Improved relations between Taiwan and the Soviet Union, commentators speculated, could be used as a threat to keep the U.S. from becoming friendly with the Chinese Communists and could be held in reserve as a new policy if the U.S. actually recognized the People's Republic.[11]

In October of 1968 Victor Louis, a Soviet journalist who was known to substitute as an envoy of his government, visited Taiwan for one week of talks with Chiang Ching-kuo. Other trips by Louis were reported but not proven. Concurrently with this Russian's unprecedented appearance in Taiwan, Professor Ku Yu-hsiu, a member of Taiwan's National Assembly and previously vice-minister of education in the Nationalist government, made an official visit to Moscow.[12] In June 1969 three officials of the Chinese

9. Ibid., pp. 67-68.

10. See *Echo of Chinese,* special issue of *West and East Monthly* (Taipei: West and East Monthly, 1966), pp. 120-121.

11. The popular Taipei newspaper *Ta Hua Wan Pao* seems to have been one of the first to advise a change in KMT policy. In April 1967 the newspaper questioned the government's traditional policy of opposing all communist countries and calling all leaders of communist nations "monsters" or "chieftains"; "there is no eternal enemy country," it continued. "We may improve our relations with other communist countries or regimes which might have helped Peking in the past so long as such improvement can help us to promote our cause of recovering the mainland and destroying Peking." This editorial was a radical departure because not only did it attack the "sacred cow" that communist countries would forever be the enemy of the "free world," but it did so without mentioning the Soviets by name. "Seeking Changes in the Delicate World Situation," *Press and Publications Survey,* 67/2367 (April 5, 1967): 17-18.

12. Harald Munthe-Kaas, "Rosy Glow," *FEER,* April 3, 1967, p. 7. In 1969 the Nationalists confirmed that Victor Louis had visited Taipei the previous year and had held conversations with Chiang's heir, but they refused to confirm rumors that the journalist had returned to Taiwan several times afterward.

Nationalist government visited Bulgaria, ostensibly for a travel and tourist convention. Sources in Taiwan denied that the trip by these three had any political implications, but outside observers believed that the decision to send these representatives to Eastern Europe could only have been made at the highest level of the Nationalist government.[13]

By 1969 KMT billboards carrying the slogan "Resist Russia" had been erased from the Taiwan landscape in another indication of the Nationalists' changing posture. A textbook entitled *A History of Russian Imperialist Aggression in China,* which outlined the Nationalists' charges against the Soviets, was dropped as a requirement for college students. Chiang Kai-shek unreservedly exonerated the Soviets of guilt in the post-1950 wars when he announced, "'without exception . . . all the wars of the last 20 years, including the War of the Taiwan Strait, the Korean War, and the Vietnam War, were started by the traitorous Maoist Communists."[14] Finally, during the Chinese-Soviet fighting at the Ussuri River, the KMT-controlled press sympathized with the Russians, describing the conflict as a "Chinese Communist invasion" of the Soviet Union. The Foreign Ministry in Taiwan dropped its contention that the disputed area was Chinese territory, perhaps more to prove that Mao Zedong was not a Nationalist and not fighting for Chinese territory than to gain Soviet favor. Just as border talks between the U.S.S.R. and the PRC were stalled, ROC paramilitary forces raided a military base in Fukien across the Taiwan Strait.[15]

During the 1970s there was supposed further evidence of a "symbolic and low-level" relationship between Taiwan and the Soviet Union. Most actions suggesting this conclusion, however, were unilateral developments having little or no official government direction. The Taiwan press printed rumors that the U.S.S.R. had expressed interest in naval or air bases on the island and that Soviet journalist Victor Louis had again engaged Chiang Ching-kuo in discussions. Subsequently, the ROC deputy minister of education reportedly visited Moscow, and other informal contacts were initiated among diplomatic personnel in foreign capitals. In 1971 ROC Foreign Minister Chow Shu-kai made the unprecedented comment that Taiwan planned trade with the Soviet Union and that private talks between Taiwan and the U.S.S.R. might occur in the future.[16] Taiwan traded with the Soviets through intermediaries in Hong Kong, according to some stories, and at the time of this writing the U.S.S.R. has been listed officially as a country with which indirect trade is allowed. In 1972 Foreign Minister Chow repeated his advice

---

13. *NYT,* June 8, 1969.
14. *FCR,* January 1979, p. 75.
15. *NYT,* June 8, 1969; Munthe-Kaas, "Rosy Glow," p. 7.
16. William Kintner and John F. Copper, *A Matter of Two Chinas* (Philadelphia: Foreign Policy Research Institute, 1979), p. 88.

that Taiwan explore options with countries hostile to China, but then the minister was abruptly fired. In 1978 rumors of ROC-U.S.S.R. discussions were raised again; this time meetings were rumored to have been held in Vienna.[17] We judge from the data that some ROC leaders persisted in their flirtation with the Russian connection up to 1978, hoping to deter the United States from extending full recognition to the PRC, and after 1978 hoping to retain some leverage over Beijing once normalization was a fait accompli.[18]

Other data suggests that although the potential Russian ally for Taiwan is useful in the salient bargaining between Taipei and Beijing, Taiwan shares the apprehension of America and China about global operations. When a few persons talked once again in late 1978 of the value of an alliance with the Soviet Union in light of America's impending new tie with China, the Chinese press in Taiwan vehemently opposed the idea. One magazine article pointed out that such an idea was tantamount to "opening the door for a wolf" and another article described the plan as a "clumsy sleight of hand."[19]

On countless occasions recently, the ROC Foreign Ministry has absolutely ruled out contacts with the Soviet Union and has fervently denied that combat ships of the Soviet Union have ever visited ROC ports. Articles in various semiofficial publications on Taiwan have joined the chorus coming from Washington and Beijing lamenting the lack of effective containment of Soviet Russia.[20] Such articles, of course, do not go so far as to admit that American-Chinese détente is an effective maneuver. Perhaps the most noteworthy signal came from President Chiang Ching-kuo in 1978. Following the May 9 border clash between Russian soldiers and Chinese civilians, Taiwan's leader made assurances that Taipei would support neither a Soviet invasion of nor any aggression against Peking.[21] President Chiang clarified his intention further in a 1980 interview. Asked how the ROC would respond to a Soviet attack on the Chinese mainland, Chiang answered, "The Chinese

---

17. Paul Hofmann, "Taiwan and Russia Said to Hold Talks," *NYT,* April 1, 1978; see also *Christian Science Monitor,* July 21, 1968 (hereafter *CSM).* The most detailed presentation of this thesis may be found in John W. Garver's study, "Taiwan's Russian Option," *Asian Survey* 18 (July 1978): 751-766. William Kintner and John Copper insist that the number of reports and the credibility of sources verifies that these ideas were in circulation in Taiwan (see *A Matter of Two Chinas,* p. 88).
18. Garver, "Russian Option."
19. "Commentary Scores Taiwan Call for Alliance with Soviet Union," *Foreign Broadcast Information Service* China (January 2, 1979): 61 (hereafter FBIS, *China).*
20. See, for example, Tan Su-cheng, "Soviet Naval Implications in the 1980's: An Analysis of the Security Factor," *Asian Outlook* 15 (June 1979): 21-26; and "What Steps Should the US Take to Contain Soviet Russia?" *West and East Monthly* 23 (November 1978): 2-4.
21. See commentary by Richard Hughes, *FEER,* June 2, 1978, p. 23.

mainland is our sacred territory and we cannot countenance aggression against it by any foreign country. The people there are our brothers, and we shall never allow foreigners to harm them. Whatever form the occupation might take, it would be imperialist aggression, and the Chinese people would fight against it to the last man. If any country attacks our brothers, it will be our enemy."[22] Chiang's position reopens the Chinese impulse to unity in the face of foreign invasion. It also shows that the ROC's anti-Communism varies to account for changing realities.

Although China is rapidly modernizing its military power and buying arms from Western Europe, Beijing is likely to remain militarily weak vis-à-vis Moscow for a long time. For this reason, Beijing remains extremely sensitive to rumors of ties between Soviet Russia and Taiwan and supports ROC citizens who rebuff their compatriots for any such suggestion. PRC spokesmen are delighted that majority opinion rejects consideration of the Russian gambit. This situation gives added impetus to the united front scheme proposed by Beijing and encouraged by the United States. It is further reinforced by America's and Japan's current leaning away from the Soviets and toward the Chinese.[23]

Other Non-Western Areas

The dynamics of superpower struggle could hardly escape the international experts in Taiwan, although most persist in casting public doubt that China and Russia are thinking differently. Taiwan, still adhering to its alliance with the United States, finds itself tethered to support of anti-Soviet measures and to indirect alliance with the PRC. Looking at Africa, for example, Taiwan editorials called for courage against Russian inroads only to find out the the PRC had joined the same crusade. In one instance, Beijing concluded that one's enemy's enemy must be a friend and acted in concert with South Africa to lend support to anti-Marxist forces in Angola. South Africa had at the same time become a major partner of Taiwan, assisting in the indirect passage of European arms to the ROC.

In the Middle East, both Taiwan and the PRC sidle up to the chief anti-Soviet Arab country, Saudi Arabia, and its Arab friends. Taiwan had counted on its diplomatic relations with Saudi Arabia during the days when the United States appeared set on derecognition. Indeed, both countries

---

22. *FCR*, August 1980, p. 4.
23. See Robert A. Scalapino, "Asia at the End of the 1970's," *Foreign Affairs* 58 (1979): 737. See also FBIS *China*, January 2, 1979, p. 1; and *CSM*, July 21, 1978, p. 11.

emphasized their trade links and interchanges of various kinds as they stressed their mutual anti-Communism. Saudi Arabia has been the ROC's biggest trading partner in the Middle East and the last important thread of international diplomatic respectability. The relationship took on paramount importance to Taiwan because of Saudi Arabia's emergence as the primary global oil power and because of that country's political conservatism. [24]

During 1979 the PRC was propelled closer than ever to countries whose general anti-Communism was leading them to fear Soviet inroads in the region. Following the U.S.S.R.-South Yemen treaty of friendship, the Chinese firmed up their connections with North Yemen, where they are assisting with major engineering and construction projects. Also, apparently with Saudi consent, the PRC concluded diplomatic relations with the gulf state of Oman. Vice-foreign Minister He Ying then made an important Middle East tour, including three states directly concerned with the Soviet grip on the Red Sea: Oman, North Yemen, and Somalia. Near the end of this year, China's ambassador in Kuwait lobbied for PRC-Saudi Arabian diplomatic relations, and "secret talks" were held, according to well-informed sources. [25] And as part of an effort to identify with the Islamic grievances against Soviet imperialism in Afghanistan, Beijing announced a decision to lift the ban on printing the Koran in the People's Republic.

Although King Khalid is not likely to compromise his deeply ingrained anti-Communism, he seems willing to tolerate cordial relations between China and other fellow Arab states, such as the United Arab Emirates, Qatar, and Bahrain. Paradoxically, Arab anti-Communism, which has provided major support for Taiwan, requires little if any Arab opposition to China. One is tempted to conclude that the Arabs do not perceive China as sufficiently Communist to endanger their societies. Anti-Communism in this region becomes the PRC's, as well as Taiwan's, best ally. [26]

Sino-American Relations

The United States and its singular superpower obligation to lead world conscience in judging the Soviet Union has also become a meeting ground for Taiwan and PRC interests. Both Chinese governments paternalistically presume to counsel Washington's naive leaders. Both encourage the U.S. to

24. *CSM,* November 2, 1979.
25. *FEER,* December 7, 1979, p. 37.
26. David Bonavia, "China on the World Stage," *FEER,* July 28, 1978, p. 23. See also Lillian C. Harris, "China's Response to Perceived Soviet Gains in the Middle East," *Asian Survey* 20 (April 1980): 364.

bolster NATO's effectiveness in Europe and both remain skeptical of the second Strategic Arms Limitations Treaty with the Soviets. The press in both Taiwan and the mainland have reported with alarm that while the SALT negotiations were going on, the Russians succeeded in surpassing the United States in military strength.[27] Both Taiwan and China support the American perception that the nonaligned nations of the Third World associate blindly with Soviets, whose actions only exploit these countries' ideological confusion and lack of experience with the Russian brand of imperialism.

This is not to say that the ROC and the PRC propose identical strategies. At this date China's foreign policy has not changed enough to accept America as a permanent comrade. The United States remains a capitalist superpower threatening potential harm to proletarian movements. It is not clear, moreover, whether China is opposed to "sham" détente between Russia and America in favor of "genuine" détente or whether China objects to détente per se.[28] Commentators in the ROC either refuse to believe that the PRC-U.S.S.R. alliance is dead or advise that solid "Free World" unity is a safer defense than befriending China to compensate for weakness in the Western camp. It seems reasonable to conclude from all of these developments, however, that the closer America comes to alliance with China, the more Taiwan's differences with Beijing will diminish. The respective ideologies become bankrupt in the face of new dangers. Chinese leaders on both sides discover that they are marching in the same parade with the United States, Japan, ASEAN, and Saudi Arabia, and it makes sense to keep in step.

---

27. *FEER,* October 5, 1979, p. 53; *West and East Monthly,* November 1978, p. 3. See also Harris, "China's Response," p. 365.
28. Samuel S. Kim, *China, the United Nations and World Order* (Princeton, N.J.: Princeton University Press, 1979), p. 478.

IV

The Hong Kong Model

The British colony of Hong Kong is perhaps best cited in a study of Taiwan's future because it is a rare case of foreign independent administration of Chinese territory. Ever since the Communist victory on the mainland, Hong Kong has stood as an anachronism to Marxist-Leninist revolutionary socialism and to Chinese nationalism. Although allowing such an anachronism to exist close to its shores compromises its principles, Beijing has never sought forcefully to repatriate the British-governed area even though the Chinese claim full sovereignty over it. Recent policies of the PRC imply that the colony's status may not change even when the lease on the New Territories expires in 1997. Chinese Foreign Minister Huang Hua has in two recent meetings with British Prime Minister Margaret Thatcher and Hong Kong Governor Sir Murray MacLehose apparently given encouragement to those hoping for continuation of Hong Kong's technical separation from the mainland. In addition to assuring that the current political status of Hong Kong will be continued, Chinese leaders have repeatedly emphasized the "Hong Kong dimension" of the mainland's plans for economic modernization.[1]

PRC Trade and Investment

Of course, Hong Kong has always been one of the PRC's main channels to the rest of the world. Chinese overall trading in Hong Kong burgeoned from $1.2 billion in 1974 to $3.026 billion in 1979. Hong Kong's exports to China grew by a massive 549 percent during 1979. Reexports from other countries through Hong Kong are also gaining and may soon equal Hong Kong's direct exports to the mainland. (Reexports reportedly increased 514 percent in 1978.) Hong Kong's importation of products from

1. Mary Lee, "Borrowed Hopes in Hong Kong," *Far Eastern Economic Review,* November 16, 1979, p. 22 (hereafter *FEER*).

the People's Republic grew an impressive 48.2 percent in 1979. Thus, Hong Kong continues to be China's most important foreign market for foodstuffs, consumer goods, textiles, and petroleum products.[2]

A source of optimism for local businessmen worried about the termination of Hong Kong's lease is the expanded investment of the PRC in Hong Kong's commerce and real estate. No one spends large sums of money buying something if he intends to appropriate it. Much tension and ambivalence thus seem to be disappearing as Hong Kong becomes the experimental laboratory for China's "rookie" capitalists to test moneymaking ideas in a laissez faire environment.[3] Hong Kong has become the location of the first joint equity ventures between Beijing-controlled interests and major Western firms. The Bank of China has recently expanded its operations in this free international trade area. It is now lending in a commercial loan syndication with a number of major international banks and is venturing to build a full-fledged finance company with thirteen sister banks and three affiliated insurance companies. The result may be that the Bank of China will become the second largest Hong Kong retail banking operation with 142 branches scattered around the islands and the New Territories which comprise the colony.[4]

In real estate the Beijing-controlled company, Kiu Kwong Investments, Ltd., has already invested heavily in Hong Kong property. In the early 1980s it expects to use joint ventures with local British businessmen to build large, high-rise villages (seventeen blocks of thirty-story buildings). Another big real estate venture involves the Bank of China and one of Hong Kong's brokerage houses in the construction of an office and shopping complex. Another Chinese joint-venture project scheduled for completion in 1984 is a residential project to be built on top of the government-owned Kowloon-Canton railway station in Shatin. China Resources Company, an important Beijing-controlled trading firm, has purchased the single largest piece of land ever offered at public auction in Hong Kong; the company proposes to develop a $6.4 billion residential town for as many as 963,000 people. These new properties, along with the many department stores and warehouses long owned by the PRC, represent an enormous accumulation of real assets by the PRC in the colony.

These developments in themselves, however, do not necessarily guarantee mainland goodwill toward Hong Kong. Many of these projects can and will be sold to the public (some even before completion) in a few years.

2. *Asian Wall Street Journal Weekly,* October 20, 1980, p. 10; April 8, 1980, p. 11.
3. Louis Kraar, "China's Drive for Capitalist Profits in Hong Kong," *Fortune,* May 21, 1979, p. 110.
4. Ibid.

China and its partners may choose to recover their profits within the decade and avoid any long-term commitments.[5]

In yet another business, Hong Kong travel operators, including the China Travel Service, have had the good fortune of becoming arrangement coordinators for the budding China tourist traffic. The PRC hopes to work more closely with the experts in Hong Kong's tourist industry and welcomes cooperation in the financing, construction, and management of hotels in China.

Hong Kong-Guangdong Ties

To take further advantage of Hong Kong's brilliant success with international enterprise, China proposes to make areas of the mainland adjacent to the colony a special export-processing zone. In this zone the PRC plans to build an industrial park of assembly plants, some of which will supply Hong Kong manufacturers. Many of the small factories have already been financed and built by Hong Kong investors hoping to escape the high costs of land and labor in the colony. The rapidly increasing cooperation between Hong Kong and nearby Chinese territories has led some analysts in Hong Kong to predict that by the end of this century one will find a thriving megalopolis stretching from Hong Kong's deep-water port through various Guangdong industrial zones and all the way to Guangzhou. Indeed, Hong Kong-Guangzhou commerce within the past two or three years has been very intense and is becoming, in a sense, a model for other cities in China. The easing of customs at the border, the direct rail route, and the increased frequency of air, hover-ferry, and passenger ship connections begun with Guangzhou in 1979 have certainly contributed to this change. A multilane superhighway, currently under construction, will further ease transportation between the two areas. City and provincial autonomy in trade and joint-venture negotiations, in development of natural resources, and in the creation of industrial and special export zones—all initiated by Guangdong in the last few years—are additional factors in the intensified activity with and ties to Hong Kong.[6]

In sum, Chinese authorities have not only adjusted to less than full sovereignty in Hong Kong, they have sought to build and profit from the metropolis which boasts of being the most capitalistic anywhere.[7] Hong Kong

---

5. Ibid., pp. 110-114; and *Asian Wall Street Journal Weekly,* April 8, 1980, p. 11.
6. James Leung, "Is China Investing in Hong Kong's Future?" *Asian Wall Street Journal Weekly,* October 20, 1980, p. 10; and Daniel Tretiak, "Hong Kong-Guangdong Commerce: Model for China's Trade Growth," *Financier,* December 1979, p. 21.
7. Kraar, "China's Drive," p. 110.

seems to have become linked to China's modernization and development. The increasing connection and penetration of China's financial institutions into the colony is convincing proof that Beijing sees little need to change the appendage character of the area. The current formula for association seems to offer sufficient rewards.

Interestingly, Hong Kong residents speculate that the ultimate agreement between Hong Kong authorities and China will call for a British commission of sorts to be contracted to administer the city but required to pay rent equal to, say, 5 percent of the administration's revenue. The position of governor would be abolished, while all the same authority would rest with a commissioner.[8] Whatever the specific terms finally reached, it would seem only reasonable that as the mainland involvement in Hong Kong persists and grows, Beijing will feel comfortable with the stability which British administration can guarantee. To force "real" Chinese sovereignty on the colony would merely serve to drive out other foreign investors and seriously cripple the territory's economy. Such a step is clearly not in the PRC's long-term interest.

Comparisons Between Hong Kong and Taiwan

Like Hong Kong, Taiwan has responded to its uncertain political future by promoting business. Of course, in Taiwan's case the PRC has not been invited to invest or trade. Taiwan's main strategy has been to demonstrate that economic ties can be just as important as if not more critical than diplomatic recognition. In the face of declining international diplomatic support, the Republic of China never had many options. Yet the decision to persevere with economics seems to have been a master stroke to achieving a safe future. Taiwan's leaders must have calculated that in the world assemblies and conference halls money would speak louder than legal technicalities and that self-determination could not easily be denied a prosperous people. In a manner of speaking, Taiwan is one of the first nations in the twentieth century to prove that a nation can be respected and can survive largely as an economic entity while it is shunned politically.

As we learned earlier, the island's trade volume with countries which denied it recognition has often grown rather than declined after derecognition. Taiwan continues trade with at least 140 countries, most of which have no embassies in Taipei. In the first half of 1979, the year of American normalization with China, Taiwan's trade registered a strong advance. If Beijing calculated to drive Taiwan into a position of negotiation through the pressure

---

8. Scenarios of this type may be found in *FEER*, January 11, 1980, p. 26.

of global diplomatic crossovers, it was badly mistaken. If reunification is to occur only through the submission of a greatly weakened ROC, then surely, as Ralph Clough states in his book *Island China,* the mainland's chances diminish with time.[9] The PRC cannot fail to be impressed by the fact that most of the countries which seek communication with Beijing have had, and continue to have, a highly successful relationship with Taiwan. Taiwan illustrates, as does Hong Kong, that Chinese can achieve industrial development and attract interest globally as technologically advanced people. Also like Hong Kong, Taiwan has always consented to the PRC's interpretation that it is Chinese territory and for that reason has continued to draw large investments from overseas Chinese. As John Fairbank noted in his fourth edition of *China and the United States,* Taiwan perches between two worlds. Politically it identifies with China's revolutionary nationalism and the general patriotism of all Chinese people; economically it has participated in the world of trade and industry which has traditionally challenged China. Mainlanders on Taiwan, in particular, appear to hope that political, social, and economic changes on the mainland will lead to a less ideological and more moderate regime there, a change which would allow eventual convergence of Taiwan and China.[10]

One credit to Hong Kong and a source of strength to the colony has been that all countries have been welcome to use port facilities and barter their wares regardless of political ideology. While the KMT in Taiwan is far from allowing this much freedom to businessmen in their country, it is remarkable that within the last year ROC authorities have permitted Nationalist Chinese to trade directly with some Communist countries of Eastern Europe. They have also allowed indirect trade with the Soviet Union, Albania, Bulgaria, and Romania. Taiwan's trade ministry urges its businessmen to participate in exhibitions, make two-way contacts between respective banking organizations, open telecommunication links, and engage in other promotional activities. A high official of the Hungarian National Bank has already visited Taiwan to establish a correspondent relationship, and many other officials from Eastern Europe have been invited to visit. Taiwan has exported yarns to Poland for several years, but this seems to be the first occasion on which Taiwan has opened its borders to Communist trade representatives. The move was justified by the "need for market diversification at a time when difficulties in international trade are cropping up worldwide." Furthermore, these countries are said to have met Taiwan's

---

9. Ralph N. Clough, *Island China* (Cambridge: Harvard University Press, 1978), p. 146.

10. A. Doak Barnett, *China and the Major Powers in East Asia* (Washington, D.C.: Brookings Institution, 1977), p. 247. See also John Fairbank, *The United States and China,* 4th ed. (Cambridge: Harvard University Press, 1979), p. 462.

condition for direct trade: "adjusting basic policy to democratic principles."[11]

Taiwan-China Trade

Perhaps more surprising to some is the flourishing but still modest exchange of goods between the two Chinas which occurs indirectly through Hong Kong merchants. People in Hong Kong estimate that PRC exporters sold approximately $45 million worth of products to Taiwan in 1978. Western European sources report that China has begun to send oil to Taiwan at special below-OPEC-level prices.[12] Within a half year in 1979 a reported 6,000% increase in value of two-way trade was due in part to China's Foreign Trade Ministry in Beijing having declared that imports of Taiwan-made items would be free of import duty since such exchange counts as interprovincial trade.[13] Authorities estimate that perhaps as much as $200 million worth of consumer goods from Taiwan entered China via Hong Kong during 1979. Added to this figure is an unknown amount of smuggling which occurs between Taiwanese and Chinese fishing boats along the China coast. Just recently, for instance, Taiwan's customs officials confiscated $2 million worth of gold bars, silver coins, and herb medicine found on six Taiwanese boats returning from alleged fishing trips.[14] Although trading with the mainland is not a public policy in Taiwan, the advantages and disadvantages have been talked about casually in Taipei during conferences of foreign scholars.[15]

Some traders in Taipei reportedly think that the ROC authorities are preparing for trade and consequential telecommunications, postal, shipping, and travel arrangements with the PRC now that official policy admits that not all Communist countries are uniformly bad. "In a few years, after the people have become familiar with the notion of trading with the Communists,

---

11. *Free China Weekly*, December 23, 1979, p. 4, and February 3, 1980, p. 6 (hereafter *FCW*); Phil Kurata, "Taipei's Bridge to East Europe," *FEER*, December 21, 1979, p. 61.
12. Mainland broadcasts have shown a keen interest in using Chinese oil to tempt Taiwan's leaders into open exchange of industrial products. See "PRC Media on Taiwan Affairs," Foreign Broadcast Information Service, *Daily Report, The People's Republic of China*, July 22, 1980, p. K2 (hereafter FBIS, *China*).
13. Taiwan buys specialty foods and Chinese medicines such as dried turtle, gensing, deer antlers, and mummified toads from the mainland. Mainlanders buy TV sets, household appliances, radios, bright clothing, and digital watches from Taiwan. See *Business Week*, October 8, 1979, p. 55; Derek Davies, "Travelers' Tales," *FEER*, November 16, 1979, p. 35; and *Christian Science Monitor*, December 13, 1979, and August 6, 1980 (hereafter *CSM*).
14. *Wall Street Journal*, January 19, 1980 (hereafter *WSJ*).
15. *Business Week*, October 8, 1979, pp. 55, 59.

conceivably Taiwan could extend trade relations to Peking on the same basis," one source is quoted as saying in Taiwan.[16]

Selig Harrison has shown us that oil may be an important link between Taipei and Beijing, even to the point of suggesting that Taiwan, with its greater technological experience, become the exploration arm of China in any future exploitation of underwater reserves. Taiwan and the PRC have through unofficial actions long ago established a reasonable demarcation line for areas to be explored by each and thus helped to prevent any future conflict arising when mainland China reaches Taiwan's technological capability for deep-water production. In the meantime, China has offered to supply Taiwan with its own petroleum when relations are improved and has invited the help of American oil firms which previously assisted the ROC in its exploration.[17]

Besides simply boosting exports, trade with the mainland is an advantage for the ROC because Taiwan's products demonstrate a highly advanced technology and productive capability. Mainlanders would surely be convinced that Taiwan is highly developed and prosperous. Peaceful economic competition with the PRC would thus reflect well on Taiwan as one of the world's foremost models for economic development. Taiwan might additionally improve its own image by exhibiting its concern for improving living standards for the people of China. At this point none of China's exportable commodities, with the possible exception of textiles, are a serious challenge to Taiwan's products. Product competition between Taiwan and China hardly seems to differ from that between Hong Kong and China. Certainly in some areas, such as agricultural equipment and techniques, Taiwan has more to offer the PRC than does Hong Kong.

Major differences exist between Hong Kong and Taiwan. The PRC does not need Taiwan as a coastal entry port. Taiwan, unlike Hong Kong, has not been a source for building PRC foreign currency reserves. Hong Kong, unlike Taiwan, does not have a government which conducts its own vigorous foreign policy nor have the administrators there ever challenged the leadership in Beijing. Hong Kong has not prepared itself militarily to the extent that Taiwan has. Nor does Hong Kong have a sizable majority of people who may wish to assert permanent independence from China, as might

---

16. Kurata, "Taipei's Bridge," p. 61.

17. According to Harrison, some people in Taiwan think that Taiwan might turn out to be the exploration arm of the mainland. A division of labor would permit Taipei to proceed with deep water exploration while Peking concentrates on its close-in areas. Harrison adds that there were no strong objections to the suggestion that there be agreement whereby Taiwan would share with the People's Republic the revenues accruing from any oil or gas produced. *China, Oil and Asia: Conflict Ahead?* (New York: Columbia University Press, 1977), pp. 121-123.

be the case with the native Taiwanese in the ROC. Finally, the colony has not been willing to risk promoting a doctrine of anti-Communism nor conditioning its dealings on strong ideological positions.

Conclusions

These dissimilarities cannot be ignored when assessing the likelihood of Taiwan's following the Hong Kong formula in its evolution.[18] Obviously, some important differences remain between Hong Kong's and Taiwan's relations with the PRC; yet the differences may not be insurmountable if current political and economic trends continue.[19] The acceptability of the Hong Kong model for Taiwan, in the view of Beijing, must certainly depend on the continued decline of the ROC's official foreign policy role in the world and the cessation of Taipei's claims to power on the mainland. Taiwan must cease to pose a military threat or a political challenge to Beijing. From one perspective, one could say that Taiwan really does not conduct a separate Chinese foreign policy since it technically has few legal diplomatic representatives. Its verbal challenge to PRC leadership has softened considerably. Taiwan's military posture may become less menacing to the mainland depending on the direction or preparedness Taiwan takes. Actually, according to some theorists, if Taiwan's level of military defense remains high, accommodation may be easier because it will not be born of weakness in the ROC position. Beijing's leaders have already demonstrated some recognition of the need for Taiwan to retain armed forces.[20]

Some effort has been made to show that Hong Kong's suitable position vis-à-vis the mainland is founded on complementary economic interests and that this pattern could be followed by Taiwan. However, economic compatibility is a much weaker case for Taiwan, and ROC authorities remain alert to

---

18. Among those who continue to suggest that Hong Kong formula is W. Klatt; note his article "Taiwan and the Foreign Investor," *Pacific Affairs* 50 (Winter 1977-1978): 644-659. Also see Michael Pillsbury, *Taiwan's Fate: Two Chinas But Not Forever* (Santa Monica: Rand Corporation, The Rand Paper Series, February 1975).

19. Conclusions were verified by foreign service staff on the Taiwan desk at the U.S. State Department.

20. Chang Pao-min's thoughts written in *Pacific Community* several years ago strongly support this conclusion. See "Taiwan Between Washington and Peking," *Pacific Community* 9 (January 1978): 194. Hungdah Chiu remains suspicious of this idea. He asserts that there will be limits to the PRC's flexibility on "peaceful unification," particularly if Taipei's policies continue to appear inflammatory. *China and the Taiwan Issue* (New York: Praeger, 1979), p. 193.

the possibilities of involuntary assistance to the mainland through economic activities.[21] Taiwan's Board of Foreign Trade, for instance, in the spring of 1980 issued a warning to ROC traders that mainland businessmen were exploiting the liberalization of trade for political purposes. The board accused leading Communist trading firms of buying Taiwan-made products in Hong Kong, relabeling them "made in Taiwan Province, People's Republic of China," and reselling the items to other countries at lower prices. Many of the relabeled items, including electrical appliances and television sets, are appearing at the Canton Trade Fair, according to the Taiwan board members.[22] An additional problem for Taiwan will occur if the PRC, which has just been granted most-favored-nation trading status by the United States, swamps the American market with large quantities of low-cost goods competitive with Taiwan's exports.

Taiwan as a quasi-independent state such as the British Crown Colony would easily make itself useful to China, much as Hong Kong has, as a processing zone or middle port between Chinese socialism and Western capitalism, particularly if the PRC's economic absorption into the West continues. China needs the superbly trained managerial personnel of Taiwan and might gain from the island's experience in economic development. What of value does the PRC offer Taiwan? Far more important than those small handicrafts and rare food items now flowing into Taiwan markets from the mainland are the vast natural resources which China has available for export. The most critical of these raw materials for Taiwan, of course, is petroleum, an item which the PRC seems quite anxious to export across the Straits.[23]

How ready is the PRC to allow the transformation of Taiwan's role with the mainland to emulate Hong Kong's? Does ideological relaxation in mainland politics provide sufficient safety for a "Taiwan, Inc." which might adopt a policy of closer association?[24] Are the challenge of economic development and modernization and the issue of strategic security more important for the PRC than the irritant of a separate Taiwan? The next chapter attempts to answer this critical question.

On the Taiwan side, we wish to know how far Kuomintang leaders are willing to go in soft-pedaling their competition with the Communist Party. Will their claims for mainland authority become gradually silenced, and will they continue to reduce their global political profile? Will the threat of

---

21. *Business Week,* March 5, 1979, p. 46.
22. *FCW,* March 9, 1980, p. 1.
23. FBIS *China,* July 22, 1980, p. K2.
24. Currently, according to Frank Ching, the Hong Kong option has very little appeal in Taiwan because only the mainland would seem to gain from such a "quasi-colonial" relationship. "The Most Envied Province," *Foreign Policy* 36 (Fall 1979): 128.

Taiwanese independence disturb the ROC's attention to economic growth and become a serious source of irritation to the PRC? Does an increasingly Taiwanese-led society challenge the government of the PRC any more than a society dominated by the Nationalists? Also, how firm is Taiwan's doctrine of anti-Communism? Is Chiang Ching-kuo's quarrel with Zhao Ziyang and Deng Xiaoping equal to his father's quarrel with Mao Zedong? Once Taiwan becomes trading partners with non-Communists and Communists alike, what are the critical reasons for continued Taiwan-China hostility? These issues are to be explored in the concluding chapter.

V

The PRC's Proposals
for Reunification

The government of the ROC has been put on the defensive during the past two years by the PRC's postnormalization initiative toward reunification. The new offers made to the ROC are more creative and more attractive than those made previously. The offers are particularly troublesome to the ROC's decision makers in light of the profound changes on the mainland and America's whirlwind entry into China's economic and military life.

Before Normalization

The intentions of the Communists in Beijing, starting with their policy of negotiating peaceful liberation in 1955, have been suspect because broadcasts were vague or mixed with derogatory language, or because the policy oscillated, or because there was obvious disagreement among the leaders. The first offers extended amnesty for repentant Kuomintang members, including Chiang Kai-shek, but continued to refer to the KMT as a "remnant clique." The KMT had a slight reprieve from these insults from 1972 until 1975, but then again Communist leaders used such terms as "tottering clique" or referred to Chiang Kai-shek as "traitor" and "political mummy." This language, coupled with frequent psychological warfare broadcasts by KMT defectors, could hardly have improved Taiwan's perception of CCP deception.

While Zhou Enlai first introduced the possibility of "peaceful liberation" as early as 1955, and later returned to themes of moderation, the official policy continued to insist that the PLA had the right to, and would probably be forced to, invade Taiwan. Zhou Enlai once suggested that "liberation" might simply mean "people are their own masters." In spite of the introduction of euphemisms such as this, the specter of military liberation of Taiwan was usually reintroduced.

After the American-Chinese Shanghai Communique, the PRC's propaganda shifted pointedly toward native Taiwanese and sought to take advantage of America's waning support for the Republic of China. For the first time, concrete steps were taken by the PRC to support their appeal, such as inviting Taiwanese businessmen from outside Taiwan to visit the Guangzhou Trade Fair or welcoming Taiwanese athletes from America and Canada to the National Games in Beijing. These moves must have been calculated merely to weaken the new leadership of Chiang Ching-kuo, for surely the PRC did not seriously intend to encourage separate Taiwanese energies. The PRC's postnormalization proposals took yet another tack. One can hardly blame Taiwan for waiting until the PRC's manner and behavior demonstrate more consistency.

The PRC's conciliation measures were usually quite vague, probably calculated to achieve propaganda victories. In 1955-1956 Zhou Enlai suggested that top KMT officials who changed allegiance might be given posts in China; even Chiang Kai-shek would be given something better than a ministerial post. Yet Beijing put forward no substantive administrative decisions to implement such proposals. As a matter of fact, many of Zhou Enlai's gestures of moderation toward Taiwan went unreported on the mainland. In 1971 Zhou was asked if Taiwan's economy would not be impoverished through absorption by the mainland. He replied that, to the contrary, Taiwan would be much better off without income taxes, with all internal and external debts abolished, and with new industrial subsidies coming from Beijing. Later, in another interview Zhou suggested that Taiwan might be like Shanghai, China's most prosperous city from 1949 to the present. No Chinese leader has clarified whether Taiwan would be a province of China or an autonomous region, but there have been references to the precedent of Tibet. To be like Tibet is hardly an exciting prospect for Taiwan.[1]

Other peace overtures in the 1970s all encouraged political defection from the Kuomintang rather than offered serious accommodation. Concurrently with Marxist-type vilification of the KMT, promises were made of no retribution against "patriots" who helped in reuniting Taiwan with the mainland.[2]

---

1. Ralph N. Clough, *Island China* (Cambridge: Harvard University Press, 1978), p. 137. For additional background on the pre-1970 proposals, see Robert G. Sutter, *China Watch: Toward Sino-American Reconciliation* (Baltimore and London: Johns Hopkins University Press, 1978), pp. 58-62. See also Robert G. Sutter, *Chinese Foreign Policy after the Cultural Revolution, 1966-1977* (Boulder, Colo.: Westview Press), pp. 10513.
2. Frank S. T. Hsiao and Lawrence R. Sullivan, "The Politics of Reunification: Beijing's Initiative on Taiwan," *Asian Survey* 20 (August 1980): 791-792.

One Year Before Normalization

During the eventful year of 1978, the PRC began hinting at significant alterations in policy toward Taiwan. In a Tokyo news conference of October 1978, Deng Xiaoping admitted that he was resigned to leaving the Taiwan issue unsettled for ten years, a century, or even a thousand years if necessary. In one overt sign of new flexibility, Beijing agreed to normalize diplomatic relations with Libya without its customary requirement that the other party break relations with Taipei.[3] Also, there appeared an unprecedented admission that Taiwan, as well as Singapore and South Korea, had achieved considerable economic success and that China should pay attention to this success. In this year also joint Taiwan-China attendance at professional and scientific conferences began. Two scientific representatives from each area met in Manila at a symposium in April of that year. Papers from both representatives were published in the symposium proceedings. Later there was a second encounter at a physics conference in Tokyo. Both of these exceptional activities reflected a change of attitudes by Chinese authorities.[4]

Events since the Chinese Communist Party's Third Plenum and Work Conference of November and December 1978 point even more conclusively toward a unification policy more genuinely calculated to provide new rapport with Taiwan. Hua Guofeng in a joint U.S.-China declaration joined the "reunification" theme, suggesting that Taiwan compatriots were similar to those in Hong Kong and Macao. Hua tried to reassure Taiwan that in the eyes of the CCP the island's status did not differ substantially from that of other Chinese areas and people outside the control of the PRC. Hua implied that in any forthcoming negotiations Taiwan's residents would have no more reason to fear a PRC invasion than would people living in Hong Kong or Macao.[5] Chinese officials dropped the phrase "liberate Taiwan" and replaced it with the term "reunification." They also spoke of "authorities" in Taipei rather than "clique." Chinese officials told a visiting U.S. congressman that on two previous occasions they had cooperated with the Nationalists in a united front and that they would not rule out a third occasion when they might cooperate with the Nationalists.[6] The PRC also said that it was

---

3. *Christian Science Monitor,* August 25, 1978 (hereafter *CSM*).

4. *CSM,* October 26, 1979. See also "Academic Conferences: First Steps toward PRC-Taiwan Reconciliation?" *China Business Review* 5 (September-October 1978): 53.

5. See Hsiao and Sullivan, "The Politics of Reunification," p. 791.

6. *CSM,* July 21, 1978. See also John Michael Newman, "The Chinese Succession Struggle: Sino-American Normalization and the Modernization Debate," *Asian Affairs* 6 (January/February 1979): 183.

prepared to begin trade with Taiwan and implemented this idea by removing any duties from Taiwanese products entering the mainland. On the eve of American normalization, Vice-premier Deng announced a new compromise of critical importance—Taiwan after reunification could retain both its government and its armed forces and remain fully autonomous. It would retain its existing social and economic system and its own security forces.[7] According to one of the U.S. senators visiting Beijing at the time, Deng suggested that Taiwan would have a status like that of Hong Kong or Macao with no pressure to change the system for as long as 1,000 years.[8] The meaning of "reunification," then, became essentially symbolic. The condition for peaceful reconciliation, that the Nationalists give up their sovereignty, was quickly coupled with the contradictory affirmation, "There would be no requirement that Taiwan disarm."[9] One might easily read into these remarks that the Nationalists were to give up only the trappings of sovereignty, nothing more. On the eve of the U.S. diplomatic recognition a message from the Standing Committee of the National People's Congress to "compatriots in Taiwan" discussed hopes to "end disunity and join forces soon."[10] In their statement, the Standing Committee members clearly turned their backs on native Taiwanese movements stating that they "place great hopes" on "Taiwan authorities." "Taiwan authorities," the message said, "have always taken a firm stand of one China and opposed an independent Taiwan. This is our common stand and the basis of our cooperation." The message concluded with a theme which was to become quite familiar in coming months, that the time had come for closer economic exchange between Taiwan and the mainland. It stated:

> Economically speaking, Taiwan and the mainland of the motherland were originaly [sic] an entity. Unfortunately, economic ties have been suspended for many years. Now construction is going on vigorously in the motherland and we also wish Taiwan *growing economic prosperity*. There is every reason for us to develop trade between us, each making up what the other lacks and create economic interflow.[11]

---

7. *New York Times,* December 3, 1978 (hereafter *NYT*).
8. *NYT,* January 11, 1979. For additional background see Newman, "The Chinese Succession Struggle," pp. 165-185.
9. *NYT,* January 10, 1979.
10. "Unit of NPC Standing Committee Message to Taiwan Compatriots," Foreign Broadcast Information Service, *Daily Report People's Republic of China,* January 2, 1979, pp. E1, E2 (hereafter FBIS, *China*).
11. Ibid.

After Normalization

Ensuing actions in 1979 combined to form a package more intriguing than ever to the Chinese in Taiwan. China pulled its troops away from the coastal areas adjacent to Taiwan and placed them nearer the Soviet and Vietnamese borders. Sporadic bombing of Quemoy and Matsu was halted permanently. Officials proposed commercial air links with Taiwan and consoled the ROC that distressed CAL aircraft unable to land in Hong Kong because of bad weather would "gladly" be accommodated at the White Cloud Airport in Guangzhou. When Philippine Airlines obtained China's agreement to initiate a Manila-Guangzhou-Beijing air route, the Chinese specifically urged them to continue regular flights to Taiwan.[12] They invited Taiwan's airline and shipping representatives to discuss a joint venture in cargo handling and said that they would like permission for PRC ships to visit Taiwan ports. They also announced plans to create a free trading zone on the coast of Fukien Province opposite Taiwan. In declaring that foreign buyers would be allowed to invest in this project, the PRC officials admitted that there was a connection between their choice of locations and the proximity of Taiwan's successful trading and processing zone in Kaohsiung Harbor.[13]

A little while later Chinese officials said they would also like to begin direct telephone and postal connections. To highlight this interest, journalists in Beijing were permitted to telephone colleagues in Taipei through Tokyo switchboards. During this same period a scientific report published in a Taiwan journal was reprinted in a PRC technical periodical. Later in the year China published for nationwide sale a collection of twenty-two medium-length novels and short stories by Taiwan authors previously printed in Taiwan.[14]

Throughout the year little negative was said about Taiwan in the exportable propaganda of the People's Republic. A survey of the *Beijing Review* issues during that year, for example, revealed only two articles dealing directly with Taiwan. Both of these only mildly attempted to link U.S.-PRC normalization with the need to open relations with Taiwan. Broadcasts to Taiwan began to picture Chiang Ching-kuo favorably. After having been maligned by the CCP as a "counter-revolutionary," Chiang was transformed into a more amenable negotiator who might assist with the "national cause." Speeches by Chiang's old classmates called him a "long-standing friend" and a potential defender of China's unity.[15]

---

12. Referred to by Frank Ching, "The Most Envied Province," *Foreign Policy* 36 (Fall 1979): 133.

13. *Far Eastern Economic Review,* January 25, 1980, p. 47 (hereafter *FEER*).

14. *CSM,* December 3, 1979, p. 2.

15. Hsiao and Sullivan, "The Politics of Reunification," p. 793.

Domestic publications and broadcasts in the People's Republic illustrate that mainland groups interpreted the "NPC Standing Committee New Year's Message to Taiwan Compatriots" as a directive for more action on their part. Forums were held in various provinces to discuss implementing "reunification," and numerous former Kuomintang personnel were gathered into public meetings.[16] Organizations such as the Meteorological Society of the PRC, citing the Standing Committee's message, urged meteorologists in Taiwan to work together with colleagues on the mainland. The Zhongshan University Alumni Association encouraged its alumni living in Taiwan to join in academic exchanges.[17] Lest the significance of these happenings be lost, it is important to recall that previously the CCP held that Taiwanese people should join with mainlanders because of their "revolutionary" desire to "join the motherland." The New Year's "Message" and postscripts to the message, as Frank Hsiao and Lawrence Sullivan have recently pointed out, called for nonpolitical rationalizations to explain why people from Taiwan and the mainland should work together.

In other domestic declarations another subtheme emerged. Taiwan's press and its businessmen were suddenly given flattering reviews. One unusual broadcast from the mainland, for instance, heralded the Taiwan press for its editorials and commentaries directed against various proposals for alliance between the ROC and the Soviet Union. The PRC editorialists agreed with the publishers in Taiwan that those suggesting such an alliance represented only a small number of people.[18] During the PRC's "February 28" anniversary speeches, which usually criticize the Nationalist oppression of Taiwanese and the parasitism of the island's "bureaucratic capitalists," speakers suddenly included all social classes on Taiwan as potential contributors to reunification. They included industrialists and businessmen "who may not even support socialism." With their know-how and experience, the speakers suggested, these people were in a position to help the cause of national reconstruction through promoting trade and economic exchange.[19]

The year 1979 was thus one of unprecedented propaganda, characterized by a radical departure from previous themes. The new themes ranged from giving KMT authorities full consideration, including the right to maintain a separate army, to broad-ranging proposals for academic and business interchanges. These same themes were repeated in 1980, louder and more specifically.

---

16. FBIS, *China*, January 10, 1979, p. H3, K2; January 12, p. G2; January 16, p. G2; January 25, pp. E20, L8; June 14, p. S3; and December 12, p. G2.
17. Joint Publications Research Service (JPRS), *Translations on the People's Republic of China,* May 18, 1979, p. 22.
18. FBIS, *China*, January 2, 1979, p. C1.
19. Hsiao and Sullivan, "The Politics of Reunification," p. 795.

Early in 1980 Luo Qingchang, head of the Taiwan group of the State Council in Beijing, became quite specific about the "peaceful" nature of reunification. The PRC, he said, would not use military means before the year 2000. Luo then praised the Kuomintang in a way that would have been unimaginable some years ago. The Kuomintang, he said, not only has a longer history than the CCP, but "there are many men of insight in the KMT." He did admit, however, that these insightful persons may not have had primary influence in the Nationalist party through the years.[20] While elevating the status of the KMT, the PRC also worked to clarify its relationship with independent Taiwanese groups living in Japan and elsewhere outside Taiwan. In the first meeting of a mainland delegation with Taiwanese in Japan during the summer of 1980, the PRC representatives emphasized that the overriding common goal must be one of a "grand national reunion." The PRC had, obviously, lost interest in using the Taiwanese independence movement to undermine the political status quo in Taiwan.[21]

In another context, an American professor visiting China reported that Chinese authorities expressed a desire for Chiang Ching-kuo to "learn from his father's lessons" and choose one of the late president's stratagems of a united front to bring about "the third Kuomintang-CCP cooperation." Were Chiang to make efforts to bring about such cooperation, "the people of the whole nation will not forget him, and his name will be written in history."[22] So the surprising rehabilitation of the ROC president continued.

Generally, little new detail was given about the nature of Taiwan's existence in its future incorporation with the mainland, except for an article in *Hsin Wan Pao,* a CCP newspaper circulated in Hong Kong. Reporting new policies toward the province of Tibet, the newspaper likened Tibet to Taiwan. For Tibet, a province with the lowest living standards, prosperity should be raised. For Taiwan, the province "with the highest standard of living in the whole country," prosperity should be "maintained." For Tibet, the policy is for as many Tibetan leaders as possible to be appointed. The policy for Taiwan is for "it to reserve the right to appoint personnel." Furthermore, the newspaper said, "It is possible that Beijing will not appoint cadres to the local administration in Taiwan, so there is no question of 'infiltration.' "[23] While the article appeared contradictory in parts, the total message that the CCP wished to entertain several kinds of special conditions

---

20. JPRS-FBIS, *China,* April 18, 1980, pp. 24-25.
21. FBIS, *China,* January 29, 1980, p. K1.
22. FBIS, *China,* January 11, 1980, L7.
23. JPRS-FBIS, *China,* June 30, 1980, pp. 956.

for Taiwan was apparent.

Encouragement of Contacts

The PRC press also made media events out of contacts which seemed to occur by happenstance. On several separate dates, for example, Taiwan fishermen were rescued at sea or had their boats repaired at mainland ports. One group of eleven was rescued by the Qidong County Revolutionary Committee; a dinner was given in their honor while they spent the night ashore. Another accident involved six fishermen from Taiwan. Rescued by Guangdong fishermen, the Taiwanese abandoned their sinking ship and returned to Taiwan via Hong Kong after visiting the Sun Yat-sen Memorial Hall and other sights in Guangdong. One group of Taiwanese fishermen became the subject of a Central Newsreel Studio documentary entitled "Compatriots' Profound Affections." The documentary portrayed the warm reception given in Zhejiang to nine Taiwanese fishermen whose boat had collided with a mainland boat. The group was shown cultural and historic sites in the area and was led on a tour of the Xihu people's commune in Hangzhou. The rescue of PRC fishermen by the Nationalists and the visit of Shanghai seamen to the port of Keelung were similarly well publicized. The seamen, who were aboard a West German freighter, were, as the mainland press chose to view it, "invited" by the Nationalist Seamen's Trade Union Council to see the sights of Keelung. They reported finding strong evidence that Taiwanese people wished for the early adoption of postal, trade, and shipping communications with the mainland.[24]

PRC athletes also made an accidental Taipei stopover. In May of 1980 a Chinese table tennis team was unexpectedly held at the Taoyuan International Airport after a typhoon made its flight to Hong Kong impossible. The head of the delegation reported that the mainland athletes quickly established rapport with airport personnel, exchanged gifts, and took photographs before their departure. "We had been thinking of holding an exhibition game," table tennis players said.[25] Indeed, the record shows that the PRC intended to solidify its reunification program through the scheme of athletic competition. Perhaps in the hope that "ping pong diplomacy" would do for Taiwan-China relations what it had for relations with the U.S., officials constantly urged that visits be made by ROC wrestlers, mountain climbers, baseball players, and even Taiwan's famous track star, Chi Cheng.[26] In March of

---

24. FBIS, *China,* June 25, 1980, p. K1; July 3, 1980, p. K2; July 8, 1980, p. K2; August 22, 1980, pp. K1, K2; August 15, 1980, p. K3; September 18, 1980, p. K1.
25. *NYT,* April 20, 1980; FBIS, *China,* June 5, 1980, p. K2.
26. FBIS, *China,* January 7, 1980, p. K1; June 5, 1980, p. K2; July 8, 1980, p. K1; August 19, 1980, p. K4; October 4, 1980, p. K1.

1980 athletes from Taiwan actually participated with Chinese athletes in an Olympic year track and field open tournament in Los Angeles. Supposedly, during the tournament four athletes from the mainland and six from Taiwan shook hands and held conversations about sports in their home areas.[27]

Cultural Efforts

Activities in the scholarly and artistic realms were also pointedly directed to support the reunification campaign. During the summer a drama entitled "The Tune of Reunion" played numerous times to large groups in Beijing. The play, which concerns a youth who returns to the mainland from Taiwan and falls in love with the daughter of a CCP cadre, was performed by the PLA Art Institute. Countless other stage plays, dance dramas, films, and television stories dealing with the themes of Taiwan-Chinese returning to relatives on the mainland were performed throughout China. A Shanghai play described the life of a young scholar from Taiwan who was preparing to return to the Chinese mainland. A television show told the touching story of a KMT military doctor and his younger relatives on the mainland. Similar stories were told by such productions as "The Returning Sailboat," "Half Screen Mountain," "Sea Woman," "Oh! Taiwan," "Land of Our Fore-fathers," "Flesh and Blood Relationship," and others. Also, through much of 1980 the Central People's Broadcasting Station continually broadcast a series of Taiwanese folk songs and instrumentals.

The mainland media also began highlighting folk festivals and art news from Taiwan and arranged to publish more books by Taiwan authors. Academicians, artists, and scientists were encouraged to seek out their Taiwan counterparts at foreign conferences. Dozens of such meetings were described in elaborate detail as if to demonstrate reunification momentum.[28]

Trade Promotion

Not only did the mainland seek to underline that communication and various social links were becoming well established, it also prominently featured budding trade connections. Articles in the mainland press frequently boasted of "big increases" in Taiwan-mainland commerce, described

27. FBIS, *China,* April 8, 1980, p. K1.
28. FBIS, *China,* July 2, 1980, p. K2; August 29, 1980, p. K1; March 3, 1980, pp. 16-17; April 16, 1980, p. B3; November 14, 1980, p. K1; August 6, 1980, p. K1; August 14, 1980, p. K1; July 7, 1980, p. K1; August 29, 1980, p. K1; July 8, 1980, p. K1; July 1, 1980, p. K1; August 1, 1980, p. K1; October 16, 1980, p. K1; October 21, 1980, p. A5; July 15, 1980, p. K1; July 29, 1980, p. K1; June 20, 1980, p. K2; June 27, 1980, p. K1.

Trade Promotion

Not only did the mainland seek to underline that communication and various social links were becoming well established, it also prominently featured budding trade connections. Articles in the mainland press frequently boasted of "big increases" in Taiwan-mainland commerce, described items on display in mainland stores, and predicted further increases in sales. Writers praised the quality of Taiwan products and told Taiwan businessmen that their products were well liked, especially because they were products made by the hands of kindred folk.[29] Translating words into action, authorities went beyond liberalizing the entry of Taiwan goods and announced that henceforth it would not even be necessary to remove "Republic of China" labels from Taiwan products. As the increase in worldwide oil prices continued to cause stress in Taiwan's economy during 1980, mainland spokesmen repeated their earnest desire to help the island with mainland petroleum resources.[30]

Political Efforts

Nor did the PRC fail to grasp at political opportunities. There were signs that more attention would be given to Sun Yat-sen as a way of indicating the mutual heritage of the KMT and the CCP. A symposium on Sun Yat-sen held in Guangzhou, for instance, heralded his immortal contributions, calling his idea of democracy the "most advanced" and "scientific." A reunion of KMT and CCP graduates of the Whampoa Academy, founded by Sun, was held for the first time in 1980. The reunion became the occasion to tie "Sun Yat-senism" and the traditions of the "two revolutionary parties" together.[31] Out of this spirit, in various political commentaries and broadcasts arose a common appeal to the Nationalists to recognize the unifying principles and put the KMT's "anti-Communism and national recovery" goals behind.

One last important feature of this period is that the PRC chose not to exploit unduly the KMT's difficulties with the Kaohsiung riots of December 1979. Critical articles carefully avoided discussing the actual demands of some of the accused Kaohsiung personalities, particularly those related to an independent Taiwan. Instead, the articles complained about the lack of

29. FBIS, *China,* July 3, 1980, p. K1; September 5, 1980, p. K1; December 1, 1980, p. K1; November 18, 1980, p. K1; June 20, 1980, p. K1.
30. FBIS, *China,* February 8, 1980, p. K1; June 13, 1980, p. B1.
31. FBIS, *China,* September 25, 1980, p. K1; JPRS-FBIS, *China,* December 1, 1980, p. 9.

democracy in Taiwan or expressed bewilderment about why persons proposing reunification negotiations would be harassed. One radio broadcast confessed being confused about why KMT authorities could make peaceful reunification the subject of talks at a Taiwan conference and then incriminate other citizens for advocating the same policy.[32] Those who study these and other recent reactions to the activists' trials in Taiwan uniformly agree that the PRC is being unusually restrained in its response, frequently brushing over the real details of the case. Responses are, at the least, far from the invective about "dictatorship" by the KMT and "oppression" which would have characterized mainland propaganda in previous years.[33]

Conclusion

Since normalization of relations with the United States, the mainland Chinese have taken a considerable variety of surprising actions to sell to Taiwan their case for reunification. In a marked departure from earlier times, the PRC has suggested numerous concessions which supposedly insure autonomy for Taiwan. It has upgraded its public attitude toward the Kuomintang party, white-washed ROC President Chiang, and urged practical, incremental steps for building trust through athletic, academic, and commercial communications. Taiwanese natives are no longer courted for their opposition to the KMT but rather for their support of stronger China-Taiwan ties. How likely is the ROC now to respond in positive ways to the mainland entreaties? Have hard-line KMT ideologies changed sufficiently? Have other developments on the mainland given Taiwan authorities reason to trust the integrity of the CCP and its many officers? The following chapters answer these questions by assessing attitudinal trends in the Republic of China.

---

32. FBIS, *China,* August 11, 1980, p. K1; *CSM,* April 16, 1980; FBIS, *China,* April 15, 1980, p. K1.
33. Hsiao and Sullivan, "The Politics of Reunification," p. 798; FBIS, *China,* April 4, 1980, p. K1.

VI

Signs of Flexibility in Taiwan

Superficially it appears that the ROC's Kuomintang has frozen its ideology in anti-Communist dogma for thirty-one years. Actually, commentaries by the ROC's leaders show that the Nationalists have been very willing to compromise on issues related to the interpretation of Communist dangers and on the specific application of anti-Communism. Nationalist Chinese reaction to the Great Proletarian Cultural Revolution in the mid-sixties, for example, illustrated that President Chiang Kai-shek fancied he could do no less than wrest control of the anti-Mao Zedong movement as a means of national recovery. In speeches of Nationalist leaders and in unofficial editorials, the KMT showed a surprising openness to forming a united front with Communism against Mao and his supporters.

Early Signs of Nationalist Flexibility

In his New Year's Day Message of 1967, for instance, President Chiang said that the Nationalists' task was to "adapt" to the "changes in the world situation." In previous years Chiang had always insisted that international changes would not alter Nationalist strategies. Then, near the conclusion of that speech, the Generalissimo appeared to suggest that the Red Guard Movement was really his own movement in disguise. He said:

> The "big-character posters" in which the Red Guards criticize the so-called "revisionism" and "capitalism" are entirely false and misleading; they are meant only to distract people's attention from the real anti-Mao sentiments aroused by the "great cultural revolution." The present renaissance of China's culture is therefore in fact the prolongation of *the Republic of China's main ideological current as expressed in San Min Chu I.* It also represents the spirit "merging military strength with the people" as accomplished in the three great revolutionary campaigns of the Northward Expedition, the suppression of the communist rebellion, and the War of Resistance Against Japan.[1]

1. *Free China Review,* February 1967, p. 86 (hereafter *FCR*). Emphasis added.

Was not Chiang saying that the Red Guards covered up a struggle against Mao in China which was basically an extension of Chiang's own policies? A further indication that this was, indeed, what Chiang had in mind could be seen in his next words, that "our [Chinese] sacred national revolutionary war" was first to "overthrow Mao Zedong." At the end of his speech, Chiang added a fresh slogan to those he typically used to close his remarks. His last words were, "Everlasting success to the National Revolution for punishing Mao Zedong and for national salvation."[2] If national revolution could be accomplished singularly by punishing Mao, then certainly a link between the KMT and the anti-Mao elements on the mainland would help to accomplish it.

Chiang's Double Ten speech that year (1967) was even more revealing. Chiang seemed determined to characterize his chief goal as suppression of Mao. "The Government," he said, "has always held that its basic responsibility is to suppress Mao, to save the nation, and to liberate the mainland people."[3] Further on, Chiang said that he wanted to bring together "all anti-Mao and anti-Communist forces" and added the explanation that the anti-Mao multitude should be welded to the anti-Communist movement.

At the conclusion of this speech Chiang clarified that he was indeed proposing an alliance or a united front with Communist forces on the mainland. Because of its crucial importance, this part is quoted in its entirety:

We shall welcome all like-minded benevolent persons and intellectuals as well as the working and farming masses—including Peng Teh-huai, Huang Ke-cheng, Liu Shao-chi, and Teng Hsiao-ping—to our united endeavors to suppress Mao and attain national salvation. *We must forego party and factional prejudices in favor of expanded political cooperation.* We must forget all past feuds and broaden the base of our revolutionary organization. *I propose an alliance of all anti-Mao forces at home and abroad* through the concentration of thought and action to destroy the handful of wandering ghosts led by Mao Tse-tung. Our revolutionary forces on the mainland must place survival ahead of victory in the political war. They must perfect their offensive against Mao while his regime is "grasping war preparations," unite in the struggle of daily life while the Mao regime is "grasping production," strengthen the puissant unity of the masses and armed forces even within Mao's so-called "great alliance," and *urge anti-Mao Communist troops to take command from Mao and Chiang-ching while the regime is engaged in its own "struggle to seize power." We should take the initiative of uniting all anti-Mao forces and should speed assistance to any anti-Mao undertaking, no matter where or when.* To meet in the rear of the enemy lines, to join forces in the front

2. Ibid.
3. *FCR,* November 1967, p. 88.

of the enemy, and to provide direct support to anti-Mao actions—these will be the vanguard of the national armed forces.[4]

There could be little doubt that Chiang wanted Mao's suppression even at the cost of "foregoing party prejudices" or, as it may otherwise be understood, at the cost of compromising the KMT's previous absolute anti-Communist stand. In 1967 Chiang extended an invitation to all Communists but Mao to join the KMT's guerrilla warfare on the mainland without penalty for their previous errors. In 1957 defectors had been expected to repent and to become anti-Communist; in 1967 nothing was said about repenting of communism; opposition to Mao appeared sufficient.

If it should not be convincing that Chiang was maneuvering to ride into Beijing on the shoulders of Communist cadres who had turned against Mao, one may see how other Nationalists continued to follow through on this line. In December 1967 Premier C. K. Yen declared that the KMT should try to implement the *tsung-tsai*'s (party director) assurance that "those who are not our enemies are our friends," to join with the awakened members of the Chinese Communist Party and employ every kind of anti-Mao struggle. Yen also predicted that once Mao was put down, his successor would combine non-Communist and anti-Communist strength. Not even the members of the Chinese Communist Party would want to "taste" the "poison of Communism and Mao-think" again, Yen said.[5] This completely reversed the earlier Nationalist position that whatever happened to Mao, his successor was bound to be fully Communist and just as belligerent as Mao. One may gather from this new interpretation that the Nationalists were hoping that those Communists disenchanted with Mao would select Chiang as their leader and Mao's successor.

In 1968 Nationalist spokesmen attempted to integrate more fully Chiang's ideas of the previous year. More frequent reference was made to the "Mao Suppression and National Salvation United Front," a term that had been originated by Chiang during Youth Day (March 29) in 1967. In January of 1968 the Nationalists decided that Freedom Day (January 23) should be transformed into a "Mao Suppression and National Salvation" rally to support action for a united front.[6]

In his New Year's message in 1968 President Chiang pointedly remarked that the Maoists were denouncing Communist cadres for following the Kuomintang's *San-min chu-i* and for making Chiang Kai-shek a "revolutionary banner." If even the Maoists recognized their opponents' allegiance

---

4. Ibid. (Emphasis added.)
5. *FCR*, December 1967, p. 82.
6. *FCR*, February 1968, pp. 75-77.

to KMT forces, Chiang seemed to be saying, then certainly these anti-Maoists were fighting for the KMT. Also, President Chiang drew attention to the fact that the anti-Maoist Communists were carrying his banner and not Liu Shaoqi's. Later in his address, the president almost seemed to be taunting mainland Communists into accepting his leadership when he said, "Every nation of the world—Democratic or Communist—must have a chief of state or president. Liu Shaoqi, whom you have called 'president,' has been missing for more than a year. Where is he now?"[7]

Chiang must have left many of his listeners bewildered by his statement that Mao advocated throwing away the "cloak of Marxism-Leninism" in favor of "Maoism."[8] It is hard to know why Chiang would want to accuse Mao of disowning Marxist-Leninist communism except perhaps as a way of proving that Chinese Communists could struggle against Mao without feeling that they were betraying communism. Chiang coupled this remark with the strongest assertion ever that it was Mao "himself" who should be "singled out" as the "sole selfish big *landlord* and *capitalist.*"[9] Now, according to Chiang, being a capitalist was among Mao's sins. What possible reason could Chiang have for making this charge against Mao except to make himself more popular with the anticapitalist, anti-Maoist Communists?[10] Through the remainder of 1968 and 1969 the Nationalists' attitude toward the mainland remained essentially the same. On October 10, 1968, Chiang said that all Communist cadres were Kuomintang in their thinking. In September that year Premier Yen said that the "anti-Mao power-seizure struggle" would gradually become an "all-around revolution and an anti-Communist movement." In 1969 the Freedom Day celebration was again turned into a rally for a "united front."[11]

The Nationalists' position underwent significant transformation largely because of changing conditions on the mainland. The Nationalists could most easily compromise on interpretations of what constituted anticommunism. Chinese communism had been but a mere unfortunate misinterpretation of Sun Yat-sen's *San-min chu-i.* Mao Zedong was perhaps unrelated to the ordinary Communist in China who had honestly but erroneously placed his enthusiasm for the *San-min chu-i* into the hands of a selfish leader. For Mao, communism was a cover under which he could seek self-glory and sell

---

7. Ibid., p. 75.
8. Ibid., p. 73.
9. Ibid. (Emphasis added.)
10. Other reports on Chiang's new policies fail to explain this difference but do refer to the puzzling change. See William Glenn, "Personal Vendetta," *Far Eastern Economic Review,* October 24, 1968, p. 184 (hereafter *FEER*); and Alex Campbell, "What's Inside the Fortune Cookie?" *The New Republic,* May 31, 1969, p. 14.
11. *FCR,* November 1968, pp. 75-76; *FCR,* October 1968, pp. 74-77.

China to Stalin, as contradictory as these two goals might seem. Chiang Kai-shek apparently carried on a personal vendetta against Mao Zedong. Once Mao had passed from the scene, there would theoretically be tremendous latitude for KMT policy toward the mainland.

What the Nationalists had not yielded and could not compromise concerned the power of the KMT government in Taiwan. To abandon their counterattack would be to cripple the top-heavy structure of predominantly mainlander rule on Taiwan. To accede to a two-Chinas formula would have the same effect. The chance to rule the whole of China was not all that was at stake. Two Chinas also endangered the Kuomintang's survival on Taiwan.

Compromise in the 1970s

During the decade of the 1970s the ROC's diplomacy was forced into the maximum test—survival in the face of UN membership for Beijing, derecognition by a majority of the world's nations and, in the end, American normalization of relations with China. That Taiwan's security remains so firm today testifies to the success of its primary policies. The ROC withheld little effort in its economic development and promotion of trade, a campaign designed to endear countless countries to Taiwan. Unless forced to do otherwise, Taiwan chose not to withdraw its membership from international organizations, conferences, and forums, even when this policy meant that representatives from the ROC might be seated in the same chambers with representatives from Beijing.[12] This strategy not only permitted Taiwan to retain some crucial mechanical links with organizations helping in the island's development, but also served to underline the point that Taiwan was a sovereign entity, whether recognized diplomatically or not. Finally, the world would be kept guessing about what response the ROC would have to the inevitable U.S.-China normalization. Somehow, as one of the world's models of development, Taiwan would endure.

---

12. The ROC apparently sought membership for itself and the PRC in the World Bank. The Republic of China was an original member of the bank in good standing and thus a member of the board of executive directors. The board was the only body authorized to make decisions regarding the membership of the People's Republic of China. Before 1980 Taiwan had a firm foothold in the bank, owning 7,500 shares and receiving loans outstanding of roughly $200 million. The ROC's minister of finance served as the China governor for the World Bank and attended the bank's meetings regularly. In light of this, it is noteworthy that in the spring of 1980 representatives of the PRC visited the World Bank to inquire about its possible usefulness to Beijing while the ROC remained on the board.

The ROC's response to China's entreaties to join the mainland and cast off the undependable Americans was consistently tough and unyielding, although on one occasion in which strategic advantages seemed complex, the KMT consented to receive military and political comrades who had been held captive on the mainland. During the summer and fall of 1975 Beijing, to dramatize its good intentions toward Taiwan, announced a phased release of Nationalist soldiers, agents, and officials captured by the PRC over the years. ROC officials had to choose either to receive their long-lost compatriots and, thus, play into Beijing's propaganda scheme, or to reject the offer at the possible expense of loyal KMT members held prisoner on the mainland. The government finally compromised and received the faithful, but only after an initial rejection resulted in disaster for some of those released by Beijing.

Post-U.S. Recognition of the PRC

U.S. recognition of the PRC was a catalytic force in moving both sides from previous, hardened positions. The ROC obviously assessed the change and cautiously began creating new formulas. The basic KMT line remained the same, that the ROC absolutely would not negotiate with the Chinese Communists and that reunification could not occur until the Chinese dropped all adherence to Marxism-Leninism. All "united front schemes" would be opposed.

Notwithstanding, some subtle factors seem noteworthy. Premier Y. S. Sun's response to Deng Xiaoping's January 1, 1979, suggestions was surprisingly mild. Reporters for the *Far Eastern Economic Review* referred to his speech as "firm but polite refusal" and a "gentle" rejection of the PRC's advances. In moderate tones Premier Sun reasoned that, of course, the ROC was not in a bargaining mood. This was not exactly a flat rejection. Furthermore, Premier Sun carefully outlined conditions admittedly far ranging which might lead to unification, and he noted that China needed "a modernized society in which all are equally wealthy and not backward communes in which all are equally impoverished."[13] This beginning introduced into ROC literature the theme that mainland China's goals for modernization and economic development could be achieved via the Taiwan mode. That Premier Sun, not President Chiang Ching-kuo, spoke at this time may also suggest that the KMT wanted a fresh approach to the problem by someone who did not carry the burden of ancestral obligation to Chiang Kai-shek.

---

13. Bill Kazer, "Gently Rejecting Advances," *FEER,* January 26, 1979, p. 26; *Free China Weekly,* January 14, 1979, p. 2 (hereafter *FCW*).

Considerable unofficial discussion of the obvious complementary features of Taiwan and China development went on during the late spring and summer of 1979. A prominent academic figure in Taiwan, Dr. Shen Chun-shan, urged Taiwan to take the initiative in providing mainlanders with some lessons about progress in the ROC. Writing in the *Wall Street Journal* of February 28, 1979, Dr. Shen declared regarding the ROC and the PRC, "Neither should try to achieve premature unification by force, nor actively or passively cooperate with a third party hostile to the other."[14] This initial statement already represented a flat contradiction to the hallowed policy of the KMT that liberating the mainland was a "sacred duty." In a different interview he said that in his view nationalists could safely accept the Communists' call for an exchange of mail and invite technical groups to visit factories in Taiwan to learn about modernization. Professor Shen also called for people-to-people contacts, especially between Taiwan students and Chinese Communist students attending universities in the United States. He said that cultural, economic, and scientific contacts were unavoidable and that a distinction should be made between the Chinese mainland government and the Chinese people.[15] The theory, of course, is that Taiwan can take advantage of its superior economic record while the people decide who can provide the better future for them.

In a similar line of thought, Taiwan's chairman of the Agricultural Planning and Development Council was quoted in a local newspaper: "If the Chinese Communists want to 'Taiwanese' their agricultural reforms, then our council is willing to contribute on a humanitarian basis and in order to improve the living conditions of our fellow countrymen."[16] The news article continued that the council's technical materials would be useful in the increasing encounters of students from Taiwan, China, and overseas Chinese communities. At about the same time, another article appeared in the local press stating that Taiwan, Hong Kong, Macao, Singapore, and the Chinese mainland could in practice organize a Chinese Common Market. "These five areas," the article continued, "can pass through a long period of

---

14. *New York Times*, April 1, 1979 (hereafter *NYT*).
15. Melinda Liu, "Taiwan's New Realism," *FEER*, July 20, 1979, p. 24. (Credit is due Ms. Liu for her persistent attention to signs of flexibility in Taiwan during 1979. However, it should be noted that frequently Ms. Liu is only able to refer to "reliable" or "informed" sources or general public comment and appears eager to see the scenario of unification fulfilled.) See also *NYT*, May 11, 1979.
16. See *FEER*, July 20, 1979, p. 23. Later the ROC Foreign Ministry denied the offer of the council for agricultural planning and development when a wire service report from Beijing claimed that the PRC welcomed the council's offer. ROC officials clarified that no offer was made and that the council was merely stating that the Communists could not be prevented from obtaining data on agricultural development from Taiwan. See *FCW*, December 1, 1979, p. 5.

economic, cultural, and social exchange and cooperation and can even naturally become a common body. This is reunification." [17]

Sports Question

Athletic competition, we noted in the last chapter, has sometimes broken down political barriers or at least imparted subtle messages of willingness to change fundamental policies. The ROC appeared by 1980 to move hesitantly toward the eventual joint participation of athletes from the ROC and the PRC in international sporting events. In April of 1979 it appeared that Taiwan would not oppose the admission of the PRC to the International Olympic Committee as long as Taipei's membership remained intact. Taipei would compromise on the issue of displaying its flag and using its anthem if Beijing were required to comply in similar fashion. This was a marked departure from the ROC's insistence in Montreal in 1976. [18] Compromise became rejection when the ROC Olympic Committee learned that the Executive Board of the IOC was asking that they be renamed the "Chinese Taipei Olympic Committee" and that they adopt an anthem and flag different from those of the ROC. Just before the winter Olympics of 1980 local Olympic leaders reversed themselves again and called for the ROC's participation regardless of the IOC's latest ruling. One member of the local committee argued that Taiwan should tolerate the decision; otherwise, Taiwan appeared to be abandoning its rights and admitting its failure. Another said, "Participation in the Olympics will make excellent publicity for the nation. So why not try to make the best of a bad situation?" [19]

There was no joint participation at the Lake Placid Winter Olympics, however, presumably because of the continuing reluctance of the ROC government to evidence weakness by compromising on a stage which receives so much world attention. Perhaps, too, the Taiwan delegation insisted on using the ROC flag and national anthem in New York in the hope that more people would be sympathetic to their cause in the "home territory" of the United States. Nevertheless, local athletes in Taiwan were determined to join in international games, and their government wished to find flexible solutions drawing less world attention, as evidenced by the first dual competition in a California invitational track meet in the spring of 1980

17. Liu, "Taiwan's New Realism," p. 24.
18. Following the IOC decision, some leaders in Taiwan urged that additional steps be taken to "prevent our country from becoming an orphan in the international community." They recommended, among other things, that the Ministry officials had stated, after all, that return to the UN was a "long-term goal" of the ROC. *FEER,* May 4, 1979, p. 25.
19. *FCW,* September 16, 1979, p. 1; and January 13, 1980, p. 2.

in which athletes from both the PRC and the ROC participated.

Other Contact

In the fall of 1979 the ROC government officially endorsed the strategy of student-to-student contact and introduced the slogan "Learning from Taipei, unification not so difficult." In a later interview on the subject, Premier Sun was quoted as saying, "We do not oppose contacts between people from Taiwan and the mainland in international activities, which are almost unavoidable. Private contacts may even help people from the mainland know better our success story in Taiwan."[20]

In view of this rationalization, it it not too surprising that for the first time since 1949 the Taiwan authorities lifted their ban on fraternization with mainland Chinese in 1980 by allowing seventeen mainland crewmen on a German merchant ship to disembark in Keelung. Local newspapers prominently displayed stories and pictures of this unprecedented event, and the government stated that mainland Chinese who arrived aboard third-country ships and wished to visit Taiwan would be welcomed. Western diplomats in the area viewed the event as an extraordinary step of accommodation by the ROC, while Taiwan officials justified their action as an effort to show mainlanders a prosperity far superior to that of the PRC.[21]

Responding partially to mainland declarations that Taiwan's expertise could be valuable to the "motherland," Taiwan officials began in 1979 discussing the idea that Taiwan could provide the technical information and economic development that the mainland needed. Premier Sun, in an address to his administration, came the closest to reflecting this idea in a public and formal way when he said, "The China we wish to unify is a modern, progressive, and democratic China, a China that can insure the life of happiness for the people and truly represent the Chinese cultural tradition. A China so unified would provide for extension of the fruits of development on Taiwan to the mainland so that our compatriots there could enjoy the same democracy, freedom, and happiness that we have."[22] The government later concluded this remarkable year by removing the ban on trading with Communist countries, including the Soviet Union.

---

20. *FCR,* December 1980, p. 3.
21. *NYT,* March 28, 1980.
22. "Unification of China Based on the Experience of Taiwan's Development: Premier Sun Yun-suan's Oral Report on Administration," *West and East Monthly* 24 (October 1979): 6. See also *FCW,* October 21, 1979, p. 1; and November 25, 1979, p. 1.

In the summer of 1980 another shift in policy occurred when Yu Kuo-hua, chairman of the ROC Council for Economic Planning and Development, suggested that trade with the People's Republic might be permissible. Answering questions from scholars at a seminar on national development, Yu said that Taiwan-made products purchased by the Chinese in international markets would prove good publicity by showing people on the mainland the prosperity of the ROC.[23] No one pressed Yu further to inquire why, if indirect trade were helpful, direct trade would not also be.

Another rather shocking event that underscores the momentous alteration of mood among people on the Nationalist side of the KMT-CCP competition was the January 1981 trip to Beijing made by Anna Chennault, a well-known lobbyist for Nationalist causes in Washington, D.C. Her meetings with Deng Xiaoping and other Communist party members were arranged by her own decision to face "reality" and certainly were not encouraged by her many Kuomintang friends. At a news conference she denied serving as a communication bridge between Taiwan and the PRC. However, it is interesting that before returning to the United States she stopped off in Taipei to see President Chiang Ching-kuo.[24]

The fact that the Taiwan government gives special instruction to its private citizens intending to participate in international conferences along with representatives from the PRC further indicates the increasing pragmatism of the Kuomintang government. Conferees may answer questions from mainland participants and may even take part in social functions with them. They are told, however, to avoid political discussion and the aggressive photographers who may seek to capture snapshots of persons from Taiwan and the mainland together.[25] From all this we see that Nationalists expect meetings with Chinese from the PRC to become increasingly common.

Political Problems at Home

Political rearrangements within the government and the KMT during the year led observers to believe that the ROC was not going to be driven to reactionary or doctrinaire extremism by the shock of U.S. derecognition. When fourteen key posts in the KMT's central standing committee were filled with new leaders, moderates in Taiwan claimed a victory. Actually, the appointments appeared to be more a victory for diversity since both moderates and conservatives were promoted. A number of relatively liberal

---

23. Foreign Broadcast Information Service, *Asia and Pacific,* July 17, 1980, p. B1 (hereafter FBIS, *Asia and the Pacific*).
24. *Christian Science Monitor,* January 5, 1981, p.5 (hereafter *CSM*).
25. Frank Ching, "The Most Envied Province," *Foreign Policy* 36 (Fall 1979): 132.

Western-trained scholars turned politicians were elevated and put into seats previously held by the party's old guard. In one promotion, U.S.-trained Chen Li-an, a young man who would discuss political and governmental matters with non-KMT politicians, was given a position previously reserved for deputies unreservedly loyal to President Chiang. Another moderate, a professor of diplomatic affairs at National Cheng Chi University, was named deputy director. Simultaneously with these new appointments, the KMT central committee approved guidelines for reforming party policy. Reforms would, they hoped, improve the electoral process and change the composition of the National Assembly and Legislative Yuan to include new and younger representatives. These developments seemed further to advance Chiang Ching-kuo's policy of infusing more, younger Taiwanese natives into government.

The KMT also seems to have realized the need to widen its political base. Chiang appears to have cast his vote with the progressive faction and in so doing to have responded to the new foreign pressures on his legitimacy by positive advances toward a more democratic system. It may have been his way of saying to mainland China that before long Beijing would have to cope with new policy makers—leaders who, while they might have less conviction for the older KMT dogma, would have much stronger support from their constituencies.

Several events in 1979 and 1980, however, defined the narrow limits of the KMT's new realism and moderation. Although the government had previously ignored unauthorized visits to China by Taiwan citizens, the daughter of one opposition legislator was placed in a reformatory to serve a three-year sentence after making a visit to China. Even though the young lady had not made any public statements during her visit, she was arrested upon her return to Taiwan. Also, a national policy adviser was dismissed from his post for traveling in China and for his statements urging cooperation between Beijing and Taipei. Although the man had been living in the United States for nearly ten years and had no policy-making role in the ROC government, his presence on the mainland was embarrassing to ROC officials. The dismissal was handled quietly—most likely to avoid speculation that Taiwan was talking with Beijing or to call the least attention to this example of disloyalty to policy. For whatever reason, authorities chose not to exploit the incident as a threat to others who would appease the Communists in like fashion.[26] Two similar cases in 1980 were the trials of Lee Ching-jung, an editor of a local magazine published in Taiwan, and Hung Chih-liang, the publisher. Hung was found guilty of subversion because of a "secret" trip to the mainland. Lee's trial followed, and he was convicted on the grounds

---

26. *FEER,* August 31, 1979, p. 24.

that his articles attempted to "propagandize for the Chinese Communists" and to promote Taiwan's "peaceful reunification" with China. Both were imprisoned.[27]

The most serious development contradicting the movement toward moderation was the government's arrest of an aging opposition leader, Yu Teng-fa. Yu was accused of carrying an article from the *Asahi Shimbun* newspaper, which reported Beijing's appeals for negotiation with Taiwan. Following this incident, a county magistrate was stripped of his duties for protesting Yu's incarceration.[28]

Analysts are still appraising the political impact of the rioting which occurred in Kaohsiung in December of 1979 and the heavily publicized trials which followed. Some observers feel strongly that this incident and the Chung-li demonstration which preceded it by several years symbolize a growing polarization in Taiwan politics, a polarization which some day could erupt into more serious political conflict. These events, some feel, have brought to the fore two distinct groups in Taiwan, generally and within the KMT. One group in their thirties and forties, it is said, are well educated, more modern, more internationally oriented, and more closely associated with the ordinary citizen. Many in this group are economically independent and need not depend on the government for their survival. These rising political activists want broader participation in Taiwan's governmental affairs and want, especially, to face more squarely the issues that divide native Taiwanese and mainland-born persons. These are people who also urge communications with the mainland and the possible formation of a new China "commonwealth."[29]

Within the Kuomintang itself, no doubt, there is no single position. Elements within the moderate wing would like to try conversations with the PRC. Some of these people had urged greater flexibility on the Olympics issue and have been promoting the expansion of indirect trade as a maneuver to test mainland integrity.[30] At the time of this writing, however, it is impossible to measure the depth of the rift and the extent to which either side, moderate or hard line, has become more persuasive. The government's censorship of additional opposition publications and its broad campaign to discredit opposition forces suggest that, at the least, Taiwan has entered a period of strict preservation of the status quo. On the other side,

---

27. See FBIS *China,* May 20, 1980, p. K1; *NYT,* April 6, 1980; and FBIS, *Asia and the Pacific,* May 2, 1980, p. B2.

28. Bill Kazer, "A Thorn in the KMT's Side," *FEER,* July 20, 1978, p. 24.

29. A description of political factions in Taiwan today can be found in the discussion edited by Victor Li, *The Future of Taiwan: A Difference of Opinion* (New York: M. E. Sharpe, 1980), p. 76.

30. Ibid.

general elections for the country's three main government bodies were held in December of 1980 without serious incident. Almost all of the leading nonpartisan candidates were elected in relative public calm. Among those elected with overwhelming majorities were Mrs. Yao Nee Chou Ching-yu, the wife of a convicted lawyer connected with the Kaohsiung riot and at the time still imprisoned. Another was Huang Tien-fu, nephew of the former legislator and publisher of *Formosa* magazine, Huang Hsin-chieh, who is also serving a prison term.

The foreign press generally acclaimed the impartiality of the elections and suggested that the Kuomintang had learned its lesson from the Chung-li demonstrations and was now sensitive to the need for strict compliance with democratic principles. Even Mrs. Yao commented, "It was a comparatively fair election."[31] It is not yet certain whether the election of these non-KMT leaders proves that harmony has returned to domestic politics or whether it shows that voices of grievance have risen to such crescendo that no KMT candidates could defeat the opposition. Surely the future strength and attitudes of Taiwan's fragmented and only partially visible opposition will be crucial in determining Taiwan's policy toward mainland Chinese. As on observer put it, the "all or nothing" attitude among certain government and nongovernment people is cause for alarm, while the Chinese talent for "compromise and improvisation" gives us hope for stability. One must further suppose that the stronger Taiwan's home base, the more likely the government is to introduce a creative foreign policy.[32]

Conclusions

In spite of serious domestic concerns which plagued ROC authorities from late 1979 through 1980, they had time to respond directly to the "reunification" campaign of the mainland. Premier Sun was recently pressed in an interview to react to China's new policies toward Taiwan. He said he agreed, "from the long-term perspective," that China must be unified.[33] Chiang Ching-kuo was asked by an interviewer why he did not invite PRC newsmen to Taiwan. Chiang replied, "The only defense I have now is the psychological defense of this nation. I cannot talk to the PRC. If I do that, I will lose my psychological defense."[34] This statement suggests

---

31. Phil Kurata, "Silence, Please, for the Election," *FEER,* August 29, 1980, p. 22; and FBIS, *Asia and the Pacific,* December 8, 1980, p. B3.
32. Gottfried-Karl Kindermann, "Washington Between Beijing and Taipei: The Restructured Triangle 1978-80," *Asian Survey* 20 (May 1980): 475.
33. *FCR,* December 1980, p. 3.
34. Li, *Future of Taiwan,* p. 80.

that Chiang may have acquired the will to seek informal arrangements with the PRC but is held back by anxiety about possible hard-line KMT reaction.[35]

ROC officials continue politely to refuse other overtures from the PRC. Taiwan refused a mainland Chinese request to take part in the international meeting sponsored by the Asian Vegetable Research and Development Center. Although several scientists from Taiwan and mainland China had jointly participated in a similar symposium in Japan the previous year, the government refused to give mainland personnel permission to make planned visits to Taiwan.[36] Also, government spokesmen refused to believe that the PRC was sincere in reviving study of Sun Yat-sen and the history of KMT-CCP collaboration after the 1911 Chinese revolution. They branded the mainland's new emphasis as a "mere gesture" and "nothing but a trick."[37] Last, in reference to the belief that China's new capitalist economic policies were transforming the ground rules of China-Taiwan relations, the ROC Ministry of Foreign Affairs said bluntly that it was not hopeful. Free economic policies would not work in the PRC, a spokesman said, because of the different nature of the society.[38]

In summary, while we must recognize the numerous imponderables in Taiwan's domestic political situation, the actions of ROC leaders have definitely changed. In the last several years authorities have adopted several new notions about international athletic competition with mainlanders, student-to-student contact, temporary, unplanned visits by unofficial mainland persons, "peaceful" competition and trade with some Communist countries, indirect trade with the People's Republic of China, and "unification by learning from Taipei." On the other hand, they remained unresponsive to spurious efforts to have the KMT drawn into talks with the mainland and fearful of any error which might be psychologically damaging. While authorities continue to make it clear that the domestic opposition has to be kept in close reins and that its efforts to give advice on reunification will be ruthlessly resisted, a moderate group continues its push for reform and flexibility.

35. Frank S. T. Hsiao and Lawrence R. Sullivan, "The Politics of Reunification," *Asian Survey* 20 (August 1980): 801.
36. FBIS, *Asia and the Pacific,* September 11, 1980, p. B1.
37. FBIS, *Asia and the Pacific,* October 9, 1980, p. B2.
38. FBIS, *Asia and the Pacific,* October 31, 1980, p. B1.

VII

Extent of Change in the PRC

There can be little doubt that the normative perspective on Taiwan holds transformations on the mainland to be pure fabrication and the PRC's new concessions to be 100 percent deceptions. Most articles and speeches discount entirely the notion that mainland reforms are causing any fundamental improvement. The Communists' offer of negotiation is merely an example of the enemy's "talk, talk; fight, fight" tactic. The proposal for "autonomy" is a smokescreen for ultimate domination and absorption—Tibet is the bitter lesson. The Nationalist experience proves that the Communist Chinese are not to be trusted.

Is there any way to test the objective truth of the Nationalists' perceptions? Is China's drive for modernization using Western capital and technology only a veneer over its profound socialism; is the democracy movement only transitory? Has the PRC kept its promises to KMT defectors? What is its record in international commitments?

Regarding China's domestic flirtation with capitalism and democracy, we need time to judge whether change is thoroughgoing or not. Diplomats, scholars, businessmen, and reporters—outside of Taiwan—seem convinced that social, political, and economic changes on the mainland are real and dramatic. Some of the past year's events, usually reported by several sources or observed in the field, bear repeating. We know, for example, that human rights, constitutionalism, right of speech, and trial by law have become commonplace topics at governmental conferences. The government seriously intends to reduce the abuses associated with the Cultural Revolution, the anti-Confucius campaign, and other various excessive programs of the Gang of Four. Chinese citizens may now talk openly with foreign tourists, and Chinese students are permitted to leave their country for study abroad.[1]

---

1. Reports that Vice-premier Deng's son, Deng Chifang, has joined the physics department of an American university attests to the surprising turnabout in traditional PRC policy. See Derek Davies, "Traveler's Tales," *Far Eastern Economic Review,* February 25, 1980, p. 23 (hereafter *FEER*).

Western styles are now acceptable; color and variety have returned to the streets of Beijing, Shanghai, and Guangzhou. Western literature, although still censored, is more freely available; churches and mosques have been re-opened, and religious leaders have been encouraged to step out publicly. Also, we can safely conclude that important political and social measures have been adopted to prevent the return of one-man totalitarianism or the gradual centralization of power into the hands of an inept bureaucracy.

Political Liberalization

The ROC has stipulated that there must be greater freedom on the mainland before reunification can occur. All available data suggests that the PRC is moving in the direction of rule by law, although not without some hesitancy.[2] The movement toward democracy and constitutionalism which characterized the last several years has been judged by the trial of the young dissident, Wei Jingsheng, and the sentencing of the Gang of Four early in 1981. Observers saw that while judicial organs were to be "independent," they were obviously still under the instruction of the Communist Party. There has been no class struggle type of campaign in China for several years now, yet the public trial of the Gang of Four seemed far from judicious to the Western mind. The mass hysteria and outcry for harsh punishment of Jiang Qing hardly seemed different from previous campaigns. People may now speak up for fixed rules, accountability of officials, and due process, but they may still risk judgment that their views are "counterrevolutionary." The Chinese people have been urged to "emancipate their minds" and to avoid "blind faith" but must definitely not do things "according to one's own whims." A few of the courageous in the PRC have asked for the whole-sale replacement of the entire Marxist system by a Western-type democracy, but usually those who wish to question the virtues of socialism feel obliged to defend "genuine Marxist socialism." Much of the very free debate which took place on Beijing's Democracy Wall has been stifled and relegated to more cloistered areas.

Measurable progress has occurred at the grass roots level of Chinese politics in the replacement of the old "revolutionary committees." Secret balloting in more than half of China's rural counties and urban districts this past year has forced the CCP to share power with members of the country's minority parties and other groups of intellectuals and independents. The new local governments not only appear more fairly elected but far more representative. Voters are reported to be much less hesitant now to put

2. Foreign Broadcast Information Service, *Daily Report, The People's Republic of China,* December 3, 1979, p. 9 (hereafter FBIS, *China*).

forward independent candidates or to conduct write-in campaigns. Reporters also believe that where elections were allegedly rigged, Beijing stepped in to rectify the situation. In one such case in Changsha, a new election was ordered after some four thousand students demonstrated against election fraud. Much of the acclaim for these positive changes comes from the mainland's own media and requires more objective proof. Party organs apparently understand the principles of grass roots democracy, for they chose to ridicule resistant cadres and to praise the newly elected independents as "more representative" and "particularly effective."[3]

The consensus among outsiders, then, is that political liberalization on the mainland is definitely recognizable but far from complete. Ross Terrill, for example, surmises in a recent article that it "looks like a de-escalation from totalitarianism (where nothing is value-free) to authoritarianism (where the power of the state is not coincident with the sovereignty of an ideology)." Moderate, constitutionalist demands may have a reasonable chance of success now, he added, but the extreme democratic demands which would bring about fundamental change in China's political system have much poorer prospects.[4] China's leaders have adopted a long-term strategy of "emancipation" in all spheres of life, yet seem less ready to tackle the political structure than other structures. Certainly, the deliberate change from "struggle" tyranny to a more predictable politics is a slow, perilous journey. Reforms may be mutually reinforcing, but the rapid modernization that China follows is likely to call for new kinds of political discipline.

Ideological Changes

Another condition raised by authorities in Taiwan is that reunification can only follow Beijing's repudiation of Marxism-Leninism and abandonment of the communes. The country is still encumbered by the requirement to pay occasional lip service to Maoist thought; and debates on domestic economic policy and foreign affairs are still obfuscated by the mass line. Current leadership, however, has demonstrated that ideology is of little concern next to China's critical anti-Soviet security requirements and the people's primary goal of achieving a modern, industrialized country by the year 2000. Common people in China now freely admit that Maoist-inspired protracted struggles were mostly a waste of time.[5] Official criticism of the

3. *Los Angeles Times,* November 16, 1980.
4. Ross Terrill, "China Enters the 1980s," *Foreign Affairs* 58 (Spring 1980): 921, 930. These conclusions were generally supported by discussions held during the March 1980 California Regional Seminar, Center for Chinese Studies, Berkeley.
5. One observer has concluded, "Today the process of myth deflation and regeneration of critical judgment has gone so far that it will be difficult to stop." Merle Gold-

excesses of Maoist ideology is no less frank. People in the United States and on Taiwan may be encouraged by the following violations of pure Maoist thought as applied Marxism-Leninism:

1. Communes are under criticism and may be modified or dismantled under a CCP policy of benign neglect. The recent trend in China's rural areas has been to curtail the operation of the "production team" either by relinquishing all accounting powers upward to the brigade or breaking the team itself down into groups of families or into single families. For the first time since the 1950s land has been redivided; and former President Liu Shaoqi, foremost exponent of the plan to reorganize communes on the basis of more private farming, has posthumously been reassessed and cleared of the most damaging accusations. One Beijing-sponsored publication was allowed to state, "The organizational form of the people's communes does not assist the accelerated modernization of agriculture and has already clearly become an obstacle. If the obstacle is not removed, how can the rural econ-omy be developed without hindrance?"[6] Another basic change in attitude is that wealthy peasants no longer must be regarded as "capitalist." The Maoist idea that the enrichment of the peasantry is antisocialist has been ridiculed in official propaganda. Peasants are now told to seek prosperity through greater use of rural free markets and through the cultivation of nongrain crops. They are to be given a stronger voice through the secret ballot and through general meetings with production team leaders to decide if they wish to be subdivided into smaller work groups.[7]

2. Overseas Chinese businessmen and financiers have been cleared of criticism and are now investing without jeopardy in areas around Shanghai and Guangdong Province as China welcomes back the bourgeoisie. Even before these most recent changes in policies, businessmen retained rights in their businesses and were entitled to a percentage of the income generated by their enterprise, though they were given only nominal control of their businesses, and the government was always the dominant partner. A small number of exceptionally wealthy Shanghai merchants continued to enjoy privilege in Shanghai at least until the Cultural Revolution. Now it may be expected that these older, enterprising executives are in line to be the heroes of the modernizing campaign.[8] The chairman of the new state corporation

man, "The Implication of China's Liberalization," *Current History* 76 (September 1979): 78. See also FBIS, *China*, October 17, 1979, p. 19.

6. Quoted from *Cheng Ming* by David Bonavia, "A Revolution in the Communes," *FEER*, March 30, 1979, p. 9. See also FBIS, *China*, November 9, 1979, p. 21.

7. Bonavia, p. 9.

8. Background on this group is provided by William H. Overholt in "Would Chiang Find Mao an Unacceptably Strange Bedfellow?" *Asian Survey* 14 (August 1974): 687. See also FBIS, *China*, March 25, 1980, p. L3.

China International Trust and Investment in Shanghai, for instance, had once owned flour and textile mills through his wealthy family. The director of the corporation is a former cigarette manufacturer in Shanghai.[9] Also, as has been noted, mainland business executives have been assigned the task of gaining business acumen in the foremost capitalist environment of Hong Kong.

3. China's youth have illustrated their disdain for Mao's *xiafang* movement by returning to the cities in large numbers. The government has encouraged the influx by introducing various schemes to expand urban employment. In a most curious departure from the past, China has offered to export manpower to Europe, the Middle East, Singapore, or Japan. Guangdong Province has been the first to propose exporting production teams to foreign areas.[10]

4. Bustling free markets have sprung up in alleys and streets around such cities as Shanghai, and consumer ambitions are correspondingly on the rise. For the first time in thirty years, elaborate displays of enticing foreign products can be seen in department store windows, and foreign currencies can be circulated to purchase these items in such cities as Guangzhou and Shanghai.[11]

5. Practically every form of business practice found in the West is now being tested in China. Mao's dictum of self-reliance and his imposition of relative economic isolation from the developed world are totally violated. China has sought financial assistance from such United Nations organizations as UNDP, UNESCO, and WHO. It has sought and obtained major loans from Japanese and American banks. Membership in the IMF and the World Bank has been approved, although it is too soon to estimate the extent of the PRC's reliance on these two organizations. The PRC has signed contracts with major American corporations involving both indebtedness and arrangements by which permanent foreign business offices are established in Chinese cities. Some contracts involve building tourist hotels in spite of previous objections to tourists in socialist China. Trade officials have announced willingness to form joint ventures, and development bonds are being prepared for purchase by foreigners.

One of China's most influential figures in its effort to secure Western investments wildly speculated that "any form of investment can be discussed, including joint ventures, compensation trading and coproduction."[12]

---

9. See Louis Kraar, "China: Trying the Market Way," *Fortune,* December 31, 1979, p. 53.
10. Richard Breeze, "Peking's People Exports," *FEER,* November 30, 1979, p. 68.
11. Melinda Liu, "Coping with the Marlboro Man," *FEER,* December 14, 1979, pp. 15, 16.
12. Statement by Ron Jiren, Chairman of China International Trust and Investment

The experiment by Fujian Province to expand its foreign trade by copying the techniques pioneered in Taiwan is another conspicuous new policy. The central government has approved the application of provincial authorities to set up an export-processing zone modeled after similar projects in the Republic of China. According to the scheme, factories would be built with foreign investment, and technology and foreigners might even be allowed to lease land for periods of twenty to thirty years. Fujian Province, which lies directly across the Strait from Taiwan, has secured three large loans from two American banks and has commissioned projects to the Carnation Company, the Bechtel Corporation, and the Parsons Corporation—all of the U.S. Additional programs for constructing a power plant are being discussed with Westinghouse and General Electric. Some joint venture factories have already begun production; some use machines imported from Taiwan.[13]

The new legal code adopted by the PRC in January 1980 underlined the firm Chinese commitment to integrate into the world market economy. The draft laws stipulated the framework of joint-venture investment, expanded existing financial systems, and created new institutions aimed at attracting multinational corporations. Provisional development corporations were encouraged to deal with private entities and with local governments of foreign countries. On the whole, the laws allowed for decentralization of decision making in production, financial planning, and management. Increasing the availability of consumer goods would place more reliance on the market mechanism and provide more economic incentive. These kinds of changes have so shocked the Western world during the past two years that Americans now refer to the "capitalization of China."[14]

To summarize, a certain shift has occurred toward the practical dismantling of true Marxist socialism. Politics and economics both have been substantially demythologized to the point that Chinese "couldn't care less about ideology." The Chinese Communist Party, yielding to the technocrats, has lost much of its day-to-day command of the government and the economy. Invigoration of representative institutions has begun, and laws are being promulgated in numerous areas to bring order and predictability to the Chinese system.[15] If economic trends continue and changes become permanent, theorists would have to agree that the People's Republic of China

Corporation, reported in *New York Times,* June 21, 1980 (hereafter *NYT).*

13. Fox Butterfield, "Chinese Region Imitates Taiwan in Search for International Trade," *NYT,* April 21, 1980.

14. Sura Sanittamont, "China's Modernization Program and Its Impact on ASEAN," *Asia Pacific Community* (Fall 1979): 58. See also Pauline Loong, "In Peking We Trust," *FEER,* May 30, 1980.

15. *National Review,* September 19, 1980, p. 1124. See also Michel Oksenberg, "China Policy for the 1980s," *Foreign Affairs* 59 (Spring 1981): 309.

has lost its claim to being a purely Marxist socialist state and instead resembles those various eclectic socialisms of Africa and Europe which combine nationalized industries with private enterprise. Furthermore, if China's leaders succeed in upholding the human rights which they say are of concern to them and if communes decline into mere approximations of prefectures, political theorists might need to question whether China can be called "Communist" any more. Authorities on the mainland may some day not see any value in labeling themselves Communists.

These trends partially fulfill nationalist objectives for the mainland. Still, we ask, how reliable are the CCP's professions of compassion toward KMT followers who decide to compromise, and can Beijing's commitment toward autonomy for Taiwan be trusted?

Treatment of KMT Defectors

Studies of the CCP's treatment of non-Communist Party members and KMT defectors in the People's Republic show that with the latter the CCP has generally driven hard bargains but honored the details of most agreements. In gaining power, the CCP often made deals with KMT opponents even when their defeat seemed certain. The arrangement with KMT General Fu Tso-yi in 1949 is the best example of this. The case of General Fu also illustrates Communist compliance with agreements with individuals who chose to betray the KMT. Later defectors were generally offered both amnesty and position without real power or authority.

Former KMT member Miao Yun-tai became the CCP's defector celebrity in 1980. Mr. Miao, said the CCP, not only was given a better life than the average government minister in the PRC but was a high appointed member of the National CPPCC Committee. The implication was that the PRC did offer KMT sympathizers a genuine "role to play" in politics. "When compared to those important officials in the party," a spokesman said, "government and army of the KMT who are currently in active service, any of the members of the advisory council can play a more significant role than Miao Yuntai, not to mention those members of the KMT Central Committee." Leaders of the CCP's "Taiwan Group" wished to let it be known, in other words, that KMT personnel would be permitted to hold important office in the PRC.[16]

Some former officers who surrendered after being promised good treatment in exchange for confession discovered that the CCP were extremely harsh in extracting humiliating confessions. Former Vice-president Li

---

16. JPRS-FBIS, *China*, April 18, 1980, p. 25.

Tsung-jen can be cited in this case. He returned to China in 1965 and was initially given safety and status in exchange for his anti-American speeches and appeals to former KMT members on Taiwan. After his initial welcome, however, we know that Li suffered abuse under the excesses of the Great Cultural Revolution.[17]

Former capitalists and businessmen who supported the Communists in 1949 fared better than is usually assumed, and certainly much better than the big landlords in rural areas, who were mostly liquidated. Businessmen were required to confess to economic exploitation—"exploitation" defined as the taking of profit. They were taxed and fined. Although reduced to maximum dependence on government because of government control, many business-men retained rights to a percentage of their profits or otherwise received government subsidies into the mid-1960s. Some wealthy Shanghai mer-chants were still observed in Shanghai before the Cultural Revolution. Most likely, these enterprising individuals encountered serious trouble during the Red Guard era.[18] Some saved their lives and are now restored to position.

The recent rehabilitation of the Taiwanese woman, Hsieh Hseuh-hung, who died in 1970, has some startling implications for Taiwan in its current effort to discover real CCP intentions. Mrs. Hsieh, a fighter for Taiwan independence, was used by the party on the mainland in its propaganda until she was criticized as a rightist in 1957 and vanished from the political scene. The resurrection of her name does not, however, constitute a mainland interest in supporting the "Taiwan independence movement" but rather sig-nals the PRC's willingness to allow autonomy in domestic affairs on the island. The rehabilitation, according to observers, is an attempt to open lines of communication with the independence advocates and to convince them that reunification will result in a measure of so-called independence.[19]

In summary, the Chinese Communists have apparently followed the Chinese tradition of reintegrating surrendered rebels into society and of emphasizing as much as possible the appearance of superior virtue and moral adherence to commitments. The CCP historically honored many of its com-mitments to groups and individuals, though it offered few commitments. When the CCP compromised with its opposition, it kept concessions subject to diverse interpretation and used vague but consistent jargon. In times of political constancy, it carried out its promises scrupulously, but domestic political surprises frequently interfered. Betrayals of sorts occurred because of unpredictable reverses of the mass line. The CCP probably believes that

---

17. Authorities now say that with regard to Li, they are letting "bygones be bygones and looking only at the present instead of the past." Ibid.
18. Overholt, "Strange Bedfellow?" p. 687.
19. *Seattle Times,* August 7, 1980.

the legalisms which dominate American thought and govern government-to-individual agreements in this country are un-Chinese and unrevolutionary. The absence of a strong legal tradition and of lawyers among the senior cadres and the experimental character of "Politics in Command" tend to undermine any confidence in negotiation with the CCP.[20]

Tibetan "Autonomy"

The PRC's record regarding keeping agreements with independent ethnic groups and foreign countries is difficult to assess but most objectively judged as mediocre. With culturally distinct but geographically remote regions, such as Tibet, the CCP initially promised autonomy and later sought full political absorption. In the Tibetan case the Chinese government agreed to "national regional autonomy" and assured Tibetans that the central government in Peking would "not alter the existing political system in Tibet."[21] The PRC has, however, always emphasized its authority over ethnic minorities and autonomous regions. Revolts in Tibet became the pretext for the PRC to declare the initial agreements nullified and brutally to crush Tibetan opposition. What followed was a thorough transformation of the political, religious, economic, and social system of Tibet—a precedent hardly reassuring to Taiwan. If Taiwan were to negotiate for autonomous status under Chinese sovereignty, the CCP would probably pressure for ambiguity in the written agreement and ambitiously pursue assimilation by using changed conditions as justification for violating its earlier promises—assuming, of course, that the general character of the CCP leadership is the same today as it was in previous decades. Vice-premier Deng Xiaoping, it should be noted, has already made general promises of autonomy for Taiwan more far reaching than those given to other regions.

International Performance

The world is relatively impressed by Chinese good faith in its international performance. Both Zhou Enlai and Deng Xiaoping have excellent personal reputations for credibility outside the circles most directly loyal to the ROC. One study of PRC compliance with its international obligations concluded that, comparatively speaking, the PRC record is outstanding. This conclusion requires rationalizing the Chinese violation of the General Conventions on Indochina, Chinese disobedience of the United Nations in

---

20. Overholt,"Strange Bedfellow?" pp. 679-699.
21. Quoted in ibid., p. 682.

Korea, the PRC's invasion of the northeast frontier area of India, and its most recent incursion into Vietnam. Apparently, the point is that the PRC can be expected to keep its promises, whether we like those promises or not.

Perhaps it should be argued that only China's post-Cultural Revolution behavior is useful for judging its current reliability. During the 1970s much of the insulting propaganda was absent; embassy skirmishes which had involved Chinese representatives abroad during the mid-1960s were unheard of; foreign businessmen bargained with the Chinese and found them reasonable. U.S. leaders traveled extensively in China and successfully negotiated normalization of relations; Chinese leaders observed the non-Chinese world through their own travel. Generally, the PRC is reaping the benefit of a very positive global image today.

UN Role

The PRC's role in the United Nations is particularly revealing. China has not sought any special advantage in the UN because of its size, population, or revolutionary heritage. The Chinese posture there has been low and generally compliant with the legal structure under which the UN operates. During many of the political contests in the various organizations of the UN, China has assumed a cautious, modest, almost self-effacing role. Opposition to issues or activities repugnant to her interests is usually expressed through nonparticipation.

China has shown active enthusiasm for many UN programs, such as the UN global conferences on population, food, environment, the law of the sea, decertification, and the status of women. Support for the establishment of a new international economic order has been firm and consistent. China has rarely used its membership in the UN to preach its revolutionary political culture. Although its verbal behavior has been somewhat revolutionary, its actual voting behavior is usually much more conservative.

Analyzed from a political viewpoint, China's UN courtship might be explained as a shrewd waiting game—never committing too much, too soon, to any issue—and therefore a function of Mao's "protracted diplomatic struggle." Short-term honeymoon or not, China is currently participating in the UN system in a positive way. Shared perception in UN chambers is that China is expanding its participation in functional sectors at a methodical pace.[22] Also, the more the Chinese invoke General Assembly resolutions in defending their policies, the more difficult it is for China to defy Assembly resolutions or to offend members' sensibilities without suffering

_____

22. For detailed discussion, see Samuel S. Kim, *China, the United Nations, and World Order* (Princeton, N.J.: Princeton University Press, 1979), p. 496.

contradiction and humiliation.

Trends in 1980

In other areas of foreign policy, the PRC has so dramatically reversed its policies that we are led to believe that it has made a long-term commitment to Western strategic interests. The complete deterioration of relations between the PRC and Vietnam and Albania, coupled with the PRC's new admiration for Yugoslavia, underscores how far the mainland has moved from the initial Sino-Soviet split.[23] Given our experience with the modern world's volatile alliances, we remain cautious about undue faith in the new singleminded, pro-West position of the Chinese. Traces of ultraleftism remain at senior levels in China, and the demotion of Hua Guofeng from the premiership late in 1980 testifies to the continued political fluctuation. The sudden pressure for Hua to retire from the Party Chairmanship without much fanfare leaves any would-be participant in mainland politics troubled and anxious. It was also disturbing to Nationalist observers to hear that Gang of Four member Zhang Chunqiao was accused of being a Kuomintang agent and traitor during his most recent trial. Apparently, people still were to believe that the Kuomintang was criminal and up to little good.[24] Press reports in the PRC continue to condemn Nationalist Chinese statements and positions.

In August of 1980 when Taiwan Premier Y. S. Sun outlined his view of the real meaning of Chinese unity, Beijing radio broadcast a lengthy repudiation. Sun, they said, was only spouting "a stream of empty rhetoric." His "speech was clearly incompatible with reality and the true facts," the broadcast added.[25] In November, Beijing radio attacked Chiang Ching-kuo's speech, saying, in effect, that the president's priorities were distorted and contradictory with the New Year's "Message to Compatriots in Taiwan." As the year closed, editorials lamented that peaceful reunification was "not going on smoothly."[26] It is somewhat surprising, given the Nationalists' unshakeable verbal adherence to the age-old themes, that the mainlanders are not more disgruntled. The fruits of PRC "united front" labors might appear about nil to Beijing.

---

23. Hungdah Chiu, "The Outlook for Taiwan," *Asian Affairs* 7 (January/February 1980): 143. See also Greg O'Leary, "China Comes Home," *Journal of Contemporary Asia* 9 (1979): 468-471.
24. *FEER*, October 17, 1980, p. 13.
25. FBIS, *China*, August 18, 1980, p. K1.
26. FBIS, *China*, November 13, 1980, p. K2; and December 9, 1980, p. K1.

U.S.-China relations in 1980 were neither smooth nor without acrimony. U.S. arms sales to Taiwan, announced at midyear, were noticed and treated as a serious aggravation by the PRC. Radio editorials warned that the consequences of these sales were "too dreadful to contemplate." Nor was Chinese indignation entirely smoothed over by the successful negotiations of Minister Geng Biao in his visit to America a little while later.[27] The selling of arms to Taiwan, one Chinese source was quoted, "will give us no choice but to settle the Taiwan question by other means."[28] The United States' decision to upgrade diplomatic privileges to the unofficial representatives of Taiwan in the U.S. in October was also strongly protested. A New China News Agency dispatch complained that the new U.S.-Taiwan agreement was an "undisguised violation" of the principles for establishing of diplomatic relations between the U.S. and China. The agreement, it said, would "hurt the feelings of the Chinese people and give rise to widespread concern and indignation in China."[29] In spite of these "feelings," however, most editorials rather calmly explained the China position and avoided any insulting terms.

Ronald Reagan's campaign statements about Taiwan were, of course, another irritant to the Chinese. Before his election Chinese officials demonstrated their dislike of Reagan by sending his emissary, George Bush, home without significant achievement. Mainland commentaries scolded Reagan for "taking a thick-headed stand."[30] After Reagan's election his reputed associate and chief Asian adviser, Ray Cline, made a so-called private visit to Taiwan for the ostensible purpose of conveying the president-elect's policies to the leadership in Taiwan. Commentators again castigated Reagan's idea of making first contacts with Taiwan and called the statements made by Cline during his travels "muddled and stupid."[31] One additional incident in 1980 gives evidence that Chinese authorities will not gloss over the "rehabilitation" of Taiwan's status by the United States. The PRC dropped negotiations to create a city-to-city relationship between Guangzhou and Los Angeles when it learned that the Los Angeles city council had ceremoniously declared "Republic of China Day" and hoisted the ROC flag. The Chinese said again that their "feelings had been hurt" and that no further consultation could occur.[32] Perhaps the most comforting note about these developments was that the responses were generally mild and polite. The Chinese position was on the whole frank but not unkind. Also, in spite of Deng Xiaoping's initial poor review of Ronald Reagan, political reporters saw hints

27. JPRS-FBIS, *China*, July 30, 1980, pp. 15-16.
28. FBIS, *China*, October 8, 1980, p. B1.
29. *Asian Wall Street Journal*, October 20, 1980.
30. FBIS, *China*, September 3, 1980, p. K1.
31. FBIS, *China*, December 4, 1980, p. U1.
32. FBIS, *China*, October 15, 1980, p. B1.

after the election that Deng was "warming up" to the new White House team.[33]

A final event of 1980, the promotion of Zhao Ziyang to the position of premier, raises more sharply the question of the character of China's future leadership. As of this writing, no evidence has been generated that would suggest that Mr. Zhao is anything other than a copy of Deng Xiaoping. His prior experience at the hands of the Red Guards was similar to Deng's. His statements, furthermore, echo Deng's remarks. The character and policies of China's future leaders are an important unknown in calculating Taiwan's future security with the mainland.

In summary, Taiwan can not yet trust the PRC's promise of autonomy. The redefinition of autonomy from Zhou Enlai's description to Deng Xiaoping's has occurred too recently and still leaves many specifics unmentioned. Domination by the moderates in Beijing has been too short; traces of revolutionary ideology still raise doubts; human rights are not yet firmly established. Still, it must also be encouraging that the Taiwan issue has become less important than the problems of Soviet advance, of development and modernization, and other goals. Pure Maoist radicalism has clearly been rebuffed; Chinese leaders seem genuinely anxious to expand democratic rights, and a mixed socialist/free enterprise system seems to be emerging. That today's mainland China has undergone dramatic change is a fact that requires reassessment of policy in Taiwan.

---

33. *Christian Science Monitor,* November 17, 1980.

VIII

Conclusions

While there remain some important differences between Hong Kong's and Taiwan's relations with the PRC, no strong reason has been found why Taiwan cannot reach the same *modus vivendi* with the mainland that the British have accomplished for Hong Kong. The acceptability of the Hong Kong model for Taiwan, in the view of Beijing, must certainly depend on the continued decline of the ROC's official foreign policy role in the world and the cessation of Taipei's claims to power on the mainland. Taiwan must cease to pose a military threat or a political challenge to Beijing. The PRC has already admitted its admiration for the economic accomplishments of the Nationalist government and promotes rapid expansion of commerce with the island as an avenue toward closer association. It has also encouraged people to think of the Hong Kong situation as an example of Taiwan's future role alongside the mainland.

These actions are consistent with the PRC's present paramount concern with economic development, a concern which has already caused major foreign and domestic reverses. Political ideologies have been thoroughly compromised by the pragmatic urgency to share in the prosperity of China's neighbors. If the PRC genuinely hopes for a positive response to their actions and reunification proposals, these must be shorn of inciting propaganda. People in Taiwan must be given more of a choice than that between a refusal interpreted as stubbornness or acquiescence interpreted as weakness. Moreover, PRC leaders must stop the constant zigzagging which has characterized domestic politics there for thirty years. The movement toward moderation will need to be clear, consistent, and long term. Reverses in the policies of expanded human rights and personal freedoms, such as the closing of Democracy Wall, are not likely to encourage people in Taiwan to put their faith in the People's Republic. As Frank Ching stated in a recent article, "Before the Nationalists will even consider hitching their wagon to Peking's star, they will have to see much better performance on the part of China."[1]

---

1. "The Most Envied Province," *Foreign Policy* 36 (Fall 1979): 128.

The Republic of China has generally conveyed a robust image reflective of economic prosperity, and it shows signs of improving its human rights record. The government showed some restraint when publications advocated contacts with the mainland, but occasionally also nervously reprimanded its critics with censorship or imprisonment. Taipei businessmen seem cautiously prepared to help the Communists develop their industry or buy raw materials from the mainland, but officials still warn of the dangers of "coexistence" and "united front tactics." The Nationalists have rebuffed all offers for negotiation or for cultural exchanges, but contacts have been necessary. Because the ROC must grasp at every opportunity to remain in touch with the international community, it has kept its membership in organizations even when Beijing joins. Taiwan's actions regarding the International Olympics illustrates the delicate maneuvers required to keep some face and dignity through a policy of flexibility.

In spite of the KMT's sometimes awkward censorship of those citizens who would risk "trial exchanges" with the mainland, it seems increasingly pulled toward ties by the force of events—i.e., the multiplication of nongovernmental communications throughout East Asia. Despite efforts to the contrary, conversations continue between academicians, scientists, athletes, and businessmen. Moderates within the KMT appear willing to contemplate some associations with mainlanders because they have confidence in the power of the respect Taiwan bears as a model of economic achievement. They find security knowing that many nations depend on Taiwan's continued membership in the world trade club.

A transformation of the PRC-ROC relationship is not subject only to the attitudes and intentions of both parties, but also to conditions beyond the control of either. It has been suggested, for example, that a positive environment of shared strategic concerns and economic interdependence is taking shape in the East Asian region and that the Beijing-Taipei association stands to benefit from this improved environment. Wherever shared strategic interests are seen, all relate to the extent by which China, Taiwan and its friends in ASEAN, Japan, and the United States feel threatened by increasing Soviet power in Central, South, and Southeast Asia. The U.S.S.R.'s link with Vietnam is, of course, the primary change in the status quo which draws these other nations together. Soviet military positions along border areas in the northeast are the ostensible secondary influence on this new, informal alliance. The mutual anti-Soviet orientation, referred to as the new "united front" by Robert Scalapino in his latest assessment of Asia, has not led to military ties but has encouraged military consultation and economic cooperation.[2] The civil hostility between the PRC and Taiwan

2. "Asia at the End of the 1970's," *Foreign Affairs* 58 (1979): 736-737.

naturally remains the weakest component in this society of common concern. One can expect the magnitude of Taiwan's international economic involvement and the PRC's planned interdependence with Taiwan's key trading partners to be instrumental in building additional, latent understanding.

These changes are all possible because internal to the East Asia region is the new perception that the risks and costs of military force have run too high and that economic development is the important issue. Particularly in the case of Taiwan and the mainland, a successful military campaign by either against the other is now extremely difficult to imagine. On the other hand, domestic economic progress and foreign trade and investment have proven to be critical sources of security. In this framework, economic planners become somewhat apolitical, professional technicians; and businessmen, knowingly or unknowingly, acquire considerable political influence. The power of these individuals is fed by regional requirements to coordinate prices, employment rates, monetary aggregates, business cycles, technical exchange, etc. The new orientation of these Asian governments thus creates interdependence and mutual interest.

The lesson of Vietnam for China may be that it needs rapidly to modernize its armed forces and not that it should explore more creative non-military leverage against Vietnam. The dominance of the economic technocrats over military establishments in China as in most of Asia may have to occur gradually. The refusal to prepare for war or to adopt a policy of belligerence as a way of defense has, after all, become commonplace in Western Europe only after considerable time and in the context of unusual supranational Common Market growth. Perhaps peaceful cross-national associations in East Asia will expand when a balance of power crystallizes mutual respect among the nations. A balance of power matched with economic interdependence is a formula in which the potential for friendship is stronger than the potential for enmity.

Not only must we question whether military affairs no longer interfere with welfarist goals in these states, we must also ask if the preeminence of economic interests isn't more likely to bring vicious competition rather than functional cooperation. Does economic interdependence produce more understanding, or greater misunderstanding and conflict? Surely economic dependence creates new tensions. Witness, for example, the relationship of Japan and the United States. Currently some commentators question whether the two are partners or enemies. In spite of the heralded benefits of Hong Kong-PRC economic interdependence, new complaints are being heard. Hong Kong businessmen are worried about the competition of the new PRC industrial zone, Shekou, situated near Hong Kong's own industrial zone. Also, Taiwan now worries about China's most-favored-nation status with the United States.

However, Since World War II economic competition has generally not been sufficient cause to sever relations or reverse friendships. At the most, friendships between nations such as Japan and the United States undergo momentary strain while advisers negotiate to remedy the problem. We might guess that this situation will continue unless the world is struck by severe depression. Apart from this kind of economic calamity, we trust the continued statesmanlike behavior of economic partners.

Economic interdependence can create a Frankenstein monster—economic boycott. One PRC option in the event it fails with its "reunification campaign" might be to seek the collapse of Taiwan's economy by pressuring foreign businessmen to withdraw from Taiwan. Threats themselves might create sufficient insecurity to frighten investors away. The PRC could also dump on the world market goods similar or identical to those produced in Taiwan to destroy ROC revenues. While this ploy is not impossible under the worst conditions, we must be reminded that no such public threat has been heard. The PRC shows no intention now of using such a tool to achieve its national goals on the Taiwan issue. Furthermore and more importantly, it probably has no capability of doing so and will not have for some time. China's scaled-down economic goals and revised purchase plans make the PRC a less significant consumer of foreign products than was originally expected. The mainland's leverage on Western businessmen, then, would be minimal, particularly as a hostile act toward Taiwan. At this point, it appears that the People's Republic needs foreign companies more than foreigners need Chinese business. China has shown amazing support of Taiwan's economic arrangements up to this point and has certainly not discouraged the dual operations of its trading partners.

Parenthetically, we have noted that the People's Republic does not need ROC trade links equal to those it has with Hong Kong. Taiwan does not represent a crucial window for Chinese products to move West nor a source from which Beijing is likely to build important currency reserves. Only the petroleum sales carry the prospect of endearing Taiwan to the mainland.

Another cautionary reminder should be that the People's Republic does not naïvely rush into the international market, ignorant of the dangers of neo-colonialism. As Bruce Cummings makes clear in his study of political economy in China's foreign policy, from the start Chinese leaders cautioned that their country might be letting the tiger in through the front door. The Gang of Four were particularly vocal about China's reentry into "colonial economy."[3] It is unlikely that the PRC's hasty economic involvement with

3. "The Political Economy of Chinese Foreign Policy," *Modern China* 5 (October 1979): 449-450.

the United States and expanded trade with Japan and Europe will be allowed to continue unabated. Chinese leaders may be expected shrewdly to perceive possible economic threats to national interest or national independence.

Finally, this study has questioned the broker role of the international businessman. While theoretically one can expect the middle-man role of foreign business executives to provide "good offices" or otherwise serve to arbitrate differences between the two sides, few of these people would presume to seek this role. Finding substantive proof of their contribution is difficult. The informal, indirect, and unintentional diplomatic role of businessmen usually defies verification. Interviews such as those conducted in Taiwan by a graduate student from the University of California, Berkeley, or those used in this study are helpful but limited.[4] Only a long-term association with many of these executives would provide accurate insight into the specific ways in which international business might undermine political barriers in the future association of Taiwan and the People's Republic of China.

Thus, directly or indirectly, interdependence of the two Chinas is neither assured nor entirely without its dangers to international peace. As this study does prove, however, the current trends in trading have apparently created new PRC respect for Taiwan and a hesitant interest in Taiwan for separating economics from politics in foreign policy toward Communist areas. Public policy camouflages the curiosity that Chinese people on both sides have for each other and the willingness to trade, share conference papers, or compete in sporting events if political goals and propaganda advantages can be removed. Contacts for business or other reasons appear to be increasing and are unaccompanied by adverse publicity or political repercussions. Hostility measured by public announcements seems increasingly restrained. The continuation of this trend portends well for a future peaceful association of Taiwan with China.

---

4. Referred to by Ching, "The Most Envied Province," p. 133.

Chronology of Events in the Reunification Campaign

Post-Korean War

1955	Zhou Enlai announces willingness to negotiate peaceful liberation.
January 1956	Zhou Enlai at People's Political Consultative Conference appeals for PRC-KMT cooperation.
December 1956	In Phnom Penh, Zhou Enlai offers jobs to those who change sides, guarantees visits of KMT kin to China, offers Chiang Kai-shek top post.
1958	PRC increases broadcasts by relatives and friends appealing to Nationalists to return to the motherland.

Red Guard Era

1959-1970	PRC literature generally insists on no peaceful resolution. Propaganda accuses U.S., Japan, and USSR of encouraging "two Chinas" scheme.
1971	Zhou Enlai outlines the prospects: Taiwan's economy would not suffer when reunited with the mainland.
	Pao Tiao Movement inspired to protect Tiao Yu Tai Islands and to exploit nationalism for the liberation of Taiwan.

Shanghai Communique Era

1972	Beijing encourages people-to-people contact, reduces criticism of Chiang Kai-shek, returns to theme of peaceful liberation, reduces criticism of "two Chinas" scheme.

	Taiwan athletes invited to national games on the mainland.

October — Ye Jianying urges Taiwan compatriots to visit mainland. Sun Yat-sen favorably revived. PRC counts on American withdrawal to assist negotiations.

1973 — Beijing continues to encourage native Taiwanese to assist with liberation. Another group of Taiwanese from the U.S. and Japan participate in Beijing sports tournament. Peace talks proposed again. Former KMT General Fu Tso-yi encourages comrades to follow his example.

Liao Chengzhi mission leaves China for Japan to visit for 33 days with Taiwanese living there.

Anti-Confucius Era

1974 — Taiwanese participate in seventh Asian Games trials in Beijing. Chiang Kai-shek called "traitor" and "political mummy," first derogatory propaganda since 1971.

Deng Xiaoping encourages people's uprising against U.S. and KMT, tells Taiwan that the U.S. is not reliable.

1975 — Taiwanese participate in the National Games in Beijing. PRC releases 293 Nationalist prisoners of war and 144 detained secret agents to win hearts in Taiwan. Propaganda refers to Chiang Ching-kuo's "tottering clique."

Gang of Four Era

1976 — Zhang Chunqiao advocates military means. Hard line criticism of U.S., USSR, and Japan repeated. Zhang tells Sen. Hugh Scott that peaceful unification with the mainland is impossible, demands that U.S. break all relations with Taiwan. Radicals stage maneuvers along the Fujian coast and attempt to build military bases in Fujian for an independent invasion.

Hua-Deng Era

1977   Beijing avoids criticism of U.S., urges peaceful solution to Taiwan issue. Taiwanese basketball players tour China.

Rep. Lester Wolff told that Chinese are not ruling out the possibility of a Third United Front.

1978   Chairman of Chinese Peasant's Party in Berkeley suggests coexistence period followed by plebiscite. PRC recognized by Libya, but does not demand derecognition of ROC.

December   Third Plenum announces change of terms from "liberate" to "reunification."

Deng says U.S. can continue investments; any settlement will take into account the island's political and economic system.

Chairman Hua in joint communique with head of U.S. Liaison Office Leonard Woodcock says arms sale to Taiwan by the U.S. does not preclude normalization.

PRC Foreign Trade Minister Li Chang in Hong Kong says there can be trade relations between Taiwan and the mainland.

NPC Standing Committee sends New Year's Message to "Compatriots."

January 1979   Deng proposes trade, postal service, shipping with Taiwan. China said to have pulled troops away from coastal areas opposite Taiwan.

Deng states that Taiwan can have full autonomy with own security forces and own government retained. PRC terminology changes from "clique" to "authorities" in Taipei.

Taiwan placing "great hopes" on Taiwan authorities.

	Sen. Barry Goldwater is invited to the PRC. Sen. Edward Kennedy is suggested as catalyst American leader for promoting negotiations.
Spring	Journalist in Beijing uses Tokyo switchboard to call colleague in Taipei direct from mainland. Deng comments to visiting senators that Congressional legislation on Taiwan impairs U.S.-China relations. Article from Taiwan magazine is published in PRC technical journal.
	Beijing official proposes commercial air links and opening of Guangzhou airport to Taiwan aircraft.
Fall	ROC Olympic committee shows interest in compromise to allow Taiwan's athletes to attend Olympic Games.
December	Beijing publishes fiction by Chinese writers in Taiwan.
January 1980	ROC Olympic athletes refused entrance to winter Olympics for wearing national flag of ROC.
Spring	Taiwan and mainland athletes jointly participate in Los Angeles track meet.
Summer	Taiwan fishermen tour mainland; PRC seamen see Keelung, Taiwan.
	Indirect PRC-Taiwan trade grows.

Selected Bibliography

Books and Documents

Angel, Juvenal L., compiler. *American Firms, Subsidiaries, and Affiliates in Taiwan,* 9th ed. New York: World Trade Academy Press, 1979.

Barnett, A. Doak. *China and the Major Powers in East Asia.* Washington, D.C.: Brookings Institution, 1977.

Chiu, Hungdah, ed. *China and the Taiwan Issue.* New York: Praeger, Special Studies, 1979.

Chay, John. *The Problems and Prospects of American-East Asian Relations.* Boulder, Colo.: Westview Press, 1977.

Clough, Ralph N. *Island China.* Cambridge: Harvard University Press, 1978.

_____. *East Asia and U.S. Security.* Washington, D.C.: Brookings Institution, 1975.

Fairbank, John K. *The United States and China.* 4th ed. Cambridge: Harvard University Press, 1979.

Haas, Ernst B. *Beyond the Nation-State.* Palo Alto, Calif.: Stanford University Press, 1968.

Harrison, Selig S. *China, Oil, and Asia: Conflict Ahead?* New York: Columbia University Press, 1977.

Jo, Yuang-hwan, ed. *Taiwan's Future.* Tempe, Arizona: Arizona State University, 1974.

Kim, Samuel S. *China, the United Nations, and World Order.* Princeton, N.J.: Princeton University Press, 1979.

Kintner, William R., and John F. Copper. *A Matter of Two Chinas.* Philadelphia: Foreign Policy Research Institute, 1979.

Leng, Shao-chuan, ed. *Post-Mao China and US-China Trade.* Charlottesville: University of Virginia Press, 1977.

Li, Victor H. *De-recognizing Taiwan: The Legal Problems.* The Carnegie Endowment for International Peace, 1977.

_____, ed. *The Future of Taiwan: A Difference of Opinion.* New York: M. E. Sharpe, 1980.

Louis, Victor. *The Coming Decline of the Chinese Empire.* New York: New York Times Book Company, 1979.

Mueller, Peter G., and Douglas A. Ross. *China and Japan—Emerging Global Powers.* New York: Praeger, 1975.

Oksenberg, Michel, and Robert B. Oxnam. *China and America: Past and Future.* New York: Foreign Policy Association, Headline Series, 1977.

Overholt, William H. *Asia's Nuclear Future.* Boulder, Colo.: Westview Press, 1977.

Peng, Ming-min. *A Taste of Freedom: Memoirs of a Formosan Independence Leader.* New York: Holt, Rinehart & Winston, 1972.

Pillsbury, Michael. *Taiwan's Fate: Two Chinas but Not Forever.* Santa Monica, Calif.: Rand Corporation, The Rand Paper Series, February 1975.

The Republic of China Is on the Move: President Chiang Ching-kuo's First Year in Office Shapes the Policies that Will Decide the Nation's Destiny. Taipei: Kwang Hwa Publishing Company, 1979.

Sutter, Robert G. *China Watch, Toward Sino-American Reconciliation.* Baltimore and London: Johns Hopkins University Press, 1978.

_____. *Chinese Foreign Policy after the Cultural Revolution, 1966-1977.* Boulder, Colo.: Westview Press, 1978.

U.S., Congress, House, Subcommittee on Asian and Pacific Affairs of the Committee on Foreign Affairs. *China and Asia—An Analysis of China's Recent Policy Toward Neighboring States: Report by the Foreign Affairs and National Defense Division, Congressional Research Service, Library of Congress, preceded by a State Department Report on Normalization Negotiations with China.* 96th Congress, 1st sess., March 1979. Washington, D.C.: Government Printing Office, 1979.

U.S., Congress, Senate, Committee on Armed Services. *China and United States Policy. Report of Senator Henry J. Jackson to the Committee on Armed Services and the Committee on Energy and Natural Resources.* Publication No. 95N-94. 95th Congress, 1st sess., March 1978. Washington, D.C.: Government Printing Office, 1978.

U.S., Congress, Senate, Committee on Foreign Relations. *Sino-American Relations: A New Turn: A trip report to the Committee on Foreign Relations.* 96th Congress, 1st sess., January 1979. Washington, D.C.: Government Printing Office, 1979.

U.S., Congress, Senate. *China. Report of the Congressional Delegation Visit of November 12-27, 1978.* 96th Congress, 1st sess., January 29, 1979. Washington, D.C.: Government Printing Office, 1979.

Whiting, Allen S. *The Chinese Calculus of Deterence: India and Indochina.* Ann Arbor: University of Michigan Press, Studies on China Series, 1977.

Williams, Jack F., ed. *The Taiwan Issue.* East Lansing: Asian Studies Center, Michigan State University Press, May 1976.

Yu, George T., ed. *Intra-Asian International Relations.* Boulder, Colo.: Westview Press, 1977.

Magazines and Newspapers

Awanohara, Susumu. "A Positive Rate of Exchange." *Far Eastern Economic Review,* December 7, 1979, pp. 73-74. Hereafter cited as *FEER.*

Barnett, A. Doak. "China's Shift: Dramatic, Ambitious—and Realistic." *U.S. News & World Report,* January 22, 2979, pp. 43-44.

Bellow, Thomas J. "Taiwan's Foreign Policy in the 1970's: A Case Study of Adaptation and Viability." *Asian Survey* 6 (July 1976): 593-610.

Bonavia, David. "Peking Plays a Waiting Game." *FEER,* May 12, 1978, pp. 26-27.

―――. "China on the World Stage." *FEER,* July 28, 1978, pp. 22-25.

―――. "A Revolution in the Communes." *FEER,* March 30, 1979, pp. 8-9.

―――. "A Sweetener from Washington." *FEER,* September 7, 1979, pp. 13-15.

Breeze, Richard. "Peking's People Exports." *FEER,* November 30, 1979, pp. 68-70.

―――. "China Woos the Arabs." *FEER,* December 7, 1979, p. 36.

"Canton 43—New Flexibility, New Era?" *The China Business Review,* May-June 1978, pp. 33-40.

Chang, Pao-min. "Taiwan Between Washington and Peking." *Asia Pacific Community* 9 (January 1978): 183-198.

Chen, King C. "Peking's Attitude Toward Taiwan." *Asian Survey* 17 (October 1977): 903-918.

Chen, Theodore Hsi-en. "Taiwan's Future." *Current History,* September 1979, pp. 71-73, 86.

Chen, Pin. "Trading with the Americans." *Free China Review,* November 1979, pp. 19-22. Hereafter cited as *FCR.*

Cheng, Joseph Y. S. "Goals of Government Expenditure in a Laizzez-Faire Political Economy: Hong Kong in the 1970's." *Asian Survey* 19 (July 1979): 695-706.

Ching, Frank. "The Most Envied Province." *Foreign Policy* 36 (Fall 1979): 122-146.

Chiu, Hungdah. "The Outlook for Taiwan." *Asian Affairs* 7 (January/February 1980): 139-147.

Choudhury, Golam W. "New International Patterns in Asia." *Problems of Communism* 28 (March-April 1979): 14-28.

Chu, Sung-chiu. "United Front Deceptions." *FCR* (June 1979): 17-20.

Clubb, O. Edmund. "China and the 'Industrialized Democracies'." *Current History* 79 (September 1980): 5-8.

Cohen, Jerome Alan. "The Year of the Law and End of Arbitrary Courts." *FEER,* October 4, 1979, pp. 53-54.

Copper, John F. "Taiwan's Strategy and America's China Policy." *Orbis,* Summer 1977, pp. 261-271.

Cummings, Bruce. "The Political Economy of Chinese Foreign Policy." *Modern China* 5 (October 1979): 411-461.

Dernberger, Robert F. "Prospects for the Chinese Economy." *Problems of Communism* 28 (September-December 1979): 1-15.

Garner, William V. "Salt II: China's Advice and Dissent." *Asian Survey* 19 (December 1979): 1224-1240.

Garver, John W. "Taiwan's Russian Option: Image and Reality." *Asian Survey* 18 (July 1978): 751-766.

Glenn, William. "Cool Line on the Senkaku 'Bandits'." *FEER,* May 5, 1978, pp. 33-34.

Goleman, Merle. "The Implications of China's Liberalization." *Current History* 76 (September 1979): 74-78, 86.

Harris, Lillian C. "China's Response to Perceived Soviet Gains in the Middle East." *Asian Survey* 20 (April 1980): 362-373.

Houn, Franklin W. "Reunification Deadlocked: The United States, China and Taiwan." *Bulletin of Concerned Asian Scholars* 9 (April 1978): 16-36.

Hsiao, Frank S. T., and Lawrence R. Sullivan. "The Politics of Reunification: Beijing's Initiative on Taiwan." *Asian Survey* 20 (August 1980): 789-802.

Hsiung, James C. "U.S. Relations with China in the Post-Kissingerian Era, A Sensible Policy for the 1980's." *Asian Survey* 17 (August 1977): 691-710.

Hsu, King-yi. "Sino-American Relations and the Security of Taiwan." *Asian Affairs* 6 (September/October 1978): 48-66.

Jacobs, J. Bruce. "Taiwan 1979: 'Normalcy' After Normalization." *Asian Survey* 20 (January 1980): 84-93.

Jao, Y. C. "The Rise of Hong Kong as a Financial Center." *Asian Survey* 19 (July 1979): 674-694.

Johnson, Chalmers. "The New Thrust in China's Foreign Policy." *Foreign Affairs* 57 (Fall 1978): 125-137.

Karnow, Stanley. "The Great Transformation in Asia, America, and the World 1978." *Foreign Affairs* 57 (Spring 1979): 589-612.

Kazer, Bill. "Gently Rejecting Advances." *FEER,* January 26, 1979, p. 26.

———. "Making the Best of Reality: Taiwan Is Promoting the Advantages of Unofficial Ties as a Way of Developing Trade." *FEER,* May 18, 1979, p. 28.

———. "A Moderate Reply to China." *FEER,* February 23, 1979.

———. "Playing for Higher Stakes." *FEER,* July 21, 1978, p. 12.

———. "A Retreat to Safer Ground." *FEER,* March 9, 1979, pp. 38-39.

———. "A Thorn in the KMT's Side." *FEER,* July 20, 1978, p. 24.

Keijzer, Arne de. "Business Catches China Fever." *Saturday Review,* March 17, 1979, pp. 32-33.

Kindermann, Gottfried-Karl. "Washington Between Beijing and Taipei: The Restructured Triangle 1978-80." *Asian Survey* 20 (May 1980): 457-476.

Kirk, Donald. "Challenging the Nationalists in Taiwan." *The New Leader* 63 (January 14, 1980): 4-6.

Klatt, W. "Taiwan and the Foreign Investor." *Pacific Affairs* 50 (Winter 1977-1978): 644-659.

Kraar, Louis. "China's Drive for Capitalist Profits in Hong Kong." *Fortune*, May 21, 1979, pp. 110-114.

———. "China: Trying the Market Way." *Fortune*, December 31, 1979, pp. 50-54.

———. "China's Narrow Door to the West." *Fortune*, March 26, 1979, pp. 63-69.

Kurata, Phil. "Taipei's Bridge to East Europe." *FEER*, December 21, 1979, p. 61.

Lampton, David M. "New 'Revolution' in China's Social Policy." *Problems of Communism* 28 (December 1979): 16-33.

Lawson, Colin. "Red Carpets All the Way for Hua." *FEER*, November 9, 1979, p. 66.

Lee, Mary. "Borrowed Hopes in Hong Kong." *FEER*, November 16, 1979, p. 22.

Leng, Shao-chuan. "Chinese Strategy Toward the Asian-Pacific." *Orbis* 19 (Fall 1975): 775-792.

Liu, K'ang-sheng. "ROC-US Relations: Questions and Answers." *FCR*, March 1979, pp. 22-28.

Liu, Melinda. "Beware the Marco Polo Complex." *FEER*, March 16, 1979, pp. 51-52.

———. "China Puts Hong Kong Investors at Ease." *FEER*, April 20, 1979, p. 42.

———. "Coping with the Marlboro Man." *FEER*, December 14, 1979, pp. 15-16.

———. "The Fifth Modernization on Democracy Wall." *FEER*, March 16, 1979, pp. 44-46.

———. "Loyalty and Rock-Bottom Terms." *FEER*, June 22, 1979, pp. 98-99.

———. "1979: One Step Backward for One Leap Forward." *FEER*, October 5, 1979, pp. 78-80.

———. "The 'Outcasts' Get Together." *FEER*, June 26, 1978, pp. 30-32.

———. "Pushing Firmly Towards Unity." *FEER*, January 26, 1979, pp. 24-26.

———. "Taiwan's New Realism." *FEER*, July 20, 1979, pp. 21-24.

———. "US and Peking Find a Way." *FEER*, May 25, 1979, pp. 73-74.

——— and Peter Weintraub. "US Catches China's Eye." *FEER*, April 28, 1978, pp. 37-40.

Ludlow, Nicholas. "China's Oil." *China Business Review* 1 (January-February 1974): 21-27.

MacFarquhar, Roderick. "The Post-Confucian Challenge." *Economist* (London), February 9, 1980, pp. 67-72.

McBeath, Gerald. "Taiwan in 1976: Chiang in the Saddle." *Asian Survey* 17 (January 1977): 18-26.

Maxwell, Bruce. "Queueing Up to Compete." *FEER*, November 16, 1979, p. 16.

Myers, Ramon H. "Couldn't It Have Been Done without Losing Taiwan?" *FEER*, March 16, 1979, pp. 46-47.

———. "Mainland No Bonanza for US Business." *FCW*, April 22, 1979, p. 1.

Nickum, James E., and David C. Schak. "Living Standards and Economic Development in Shanghai and Taiwan." *The China Quarterly,* March 1979, pp. 25-49.

Nussbaum, Bruce. "Hopes that Sino-US Trade Will Reach US $5 Billion by 1981." *FEER,* March 16, 1979, pp. 47-49.

O'Leary, Greg. "China Comes Home: The Reintegration of China into the World Economy." *Journal of Contemporary Asia* 9 (1979): 455-477.

O'Leary, James. "Envisioning Interdependence: Perspectives on Future World Orders." *Orbis* 22 (Fall 1978): 503-537.

Okita, Saburo. "Japan, China, and the United States." *Foreign Affairs* 57 (Summer 1979): 1090-1110.

Oksenberg, Michel. "China Policy for the 1980's." *Foreign Affairs* 59 (Spring 1981): 304-322.

Overholt, William H. "Would Chiang Find Mao an Unacceptably Strange Bedfellow?" *Asian Survey* 14 (August 1974): 679-699.

Pons, Philippe. "The Taiwan Dilemma." *Atlas World Press in Review,* December 1976, pp. 15-18.

Prybla, Jan S. "United States Trade with China." *Current History* 76 (May/June 1979): 209-213, 222.

Ravenal, Earl C. "The New Strategic Balance in Asia." *Asia Pacific Community,* Fall 1978, pp. 92-116.

Rowan, Roy. "Taiwan Gears Up to Go It Alone." *Fortune,* February 12, 1979, pp. 72-77.

Sanittamont, Sura. "China's Modernization Program and Its Impact on ASEAN." *Asia Pacific Community,* Fall 1979, pp. 56-71.

Scalapino, Robert A. "Asia at the End of the 1970s." *Foreign Affairs* 58: 693-737.

Schubert, James N. "Toward a 'Working Peace System' in Asia: Organizational Growth and State Participation in Asian Regionalism." *International Organization* 32 (Spring 1978): 425-462.

_____. "US Aides Face a New Life in Taiwan." *New York Times,* March 30, 1979.

Sit, Victor. "A Challenge for Hong Kong." *FEER,* February 1, 1980, pp. 48-51.

Srodes, James. "Easing the Way for China Deals." *FEER,* November 23, 1979, p. 66.

Starr, John Bryan. "China's Economic Outreach." *Current History* 76 (September 1979): 49-51, 87.

_____. "Taiwan: New Ways Back to the Mainland." *The Interdependent* 6 (May 1979): 7.

Subhan, Malcolm. "Peking's Winning Ways in Europe." *FEER,* December 7, 1979, p. 74.

_____. "Success in the First Round." *FEER,* December 14, 1979, pp. 109-110.

Sutton, Horace. "China: Rushing to Join the World." *Saturday Review,* March 17, 1979, pp. 16-31.

Tan, Su-cheng. "Soviet Naval Implications in the 1980's: An Analysis of the Security Factor." *Asian Outlook* 15 (June 1979): 21-26.

Terrill, Ross. "China Enters the 1980's." *Foreign Affairs* 58 (Spring 1980): 920-935.

Thompson, Thomas N. "Taiwan's Ambiguous Destiny." *Asian Survey* 16 (July 1976): 611-619.

Tretiak, Daniel. "Hong Kong-Guangdong Commerce: Model for China's Trade Growth." *Financier*, December 1979, pp. 18-22.

Ts'ai, Ch'ing-yuan. "Confident Investors." *FCR*, January 1978, pp. 24-26.

———. "Friends from ASEAN." *FCR*, February 1978, pp. 23-25.

———. "Record Year for the Economy." *FCR*, January 1979, pp. 19-23.

Unger, Leonard. "Derecognition Worked." *Foreign Policy* 36 (Fall 1979): 105-121.

Warner, Denis. "Taiwan: An Unmarried Country." *Atlantic Monthly*, January 1980, pp. 14-21.

"What Steps Should the US Take to Contain Soviet Russia?—A Studied Opinion by the Magazine Publishers Association of the Republic of China." *West and East Monthly* 23 (November 1978): 2-4.

Yang, Ming-che. "Double Digit Growth." *FCR*, August 1978, pp. 9-14.

———. "Stronger than Ever." *FCR*, October 1979, pp. 9-12.

———. "With Dignity and Vigor." *FCR*, January 1979, pp. 9-18.

INSTITUTE OF EAST ASIAN STUDIES PUBLICATIONS SERIES

China Research Monographs

1. James R. Townsend. *The Revolutionization of Chinese Youth: A Study of Chung-Kuo Ch'ing-nien*, 1967 ($3.00)

2. Richard Baum and Frederick C. Teiwes. *Ssu-Ch'ing: The Socialist Education Movement of 1962–1966*, 1968*

3. Robert Rinden and Roxane Witke. *The Red Flag Waves: A Guide to the Hung-ch'i p'iao-p'iao Collection*, 1968 ($4.50)

4. Klaus Mehnert. *Peking and the New Left: At Home and Abroad*, 1969*

5. George T. Yu. *China and Tanzania: A Study in Cooperative Interaction*, 1970

6. David D. Barrett. *Dixie Mission: The United States Army Observer Group in Yenam, 1944*, 1970 ($4.00)

7. John S. Service. *The Amerasia Papers: Some Problems in the History of US–China Relations*, 1971 ($4.00)

8. Daniel D. Lovelace. *China and "People's War" in Thailand, 1964–1969*, 1972*

9. Jonathan Porter. *Tseng Kuo-fan's Private Bureaucracy*, 1972 ($5.00)

10. Derek J. Waller. *The Kiangsi Soviet Republic: Mao and the National Congresses of 1931 and 1934*, 1973 ($5.00)

11. T. A. Bisson. *Yenan in June 1937: Talks with the Communist Leaders*, 1973 ($5.00)

12. Gordon Bennett. *Yundong: Mass Campaigns in Chinese Communist Leadership*, 1976 ($4.50)

sp. John B. Starr and Nancy A. Dyer. *Post-Liberation Works of Mao Zedong: A Bibliography and Index*, 1976 ($7.50)

13. Philip Huang, Lynda Bell, and Kathy Walker. *Chinese Communists and Rural Society, 1927–1934*, 1978 ($5.00)

14. Jeffrey G. Barlow. *Sun Yat-sen and the French, 1900–1908*, 1979 ($4.00)

15. Joyce K. Kallgren, Editor. *The People's Republic of China after Thirty Years: An Overview*, 1979 ($5.00)

16. Tong-eng Wang. *Economic Policies and Price Stability in China*, 1980 ($8.00)

17. Frederic Wakeman, Jr., Editor. *Ming and Qing Historical Studies in the People's Republic of China*, 1981 ($8.00)

18. Robert E. Bedeski. *State-Building in Modern China: The Kuomintang in the Prewar Period*, 1981 ($8.00)

19. Stanley Rosen. *The Role of Sent-Down Youth in the Chinese Cultural Revolution: The Case of Guangzhou*, 1981 ($8.00)

21. James Cole. *The People Versus the Taipings: Bao Lisheng's "Righteous Army of Dongan,"* 1981 ($6.00)

22. Dan C. Sanford. *The Future Association of Taiwan with the People's Republic of China,* 1982 ($8.00)

23. A. James Gregor. *Ideology and Development: Sun Yat-sen and the Economic History of Taiwan*, 1982 ($8.00)

---

*Out of print. May be ordered from University Microfilms, 300 North Zeeb Road, Ann Arbor, Michigan 48106.